Oct 2002.

Whose Life is it Anyway?

D0582562

Whose Life is it Anyway?

A lifeline in a stress-soaked world

Neil Hood

Authentic
LIFESTYLE

First published in 2002 by Authentic Lifestyle

08 07 06 05 04 03 02   7 6 5 4 3 2 1

Authentic Lifestyle is an imprint of Authentic Media
PO Box 300, Carlisle, Cumbria, CA3 0QS, UK
Box 1047, Waynesboro, GA 30830-2047, USA
www.paternoster-publishing.com

British Library Cataloguing in Publication Data
A catalogue record for this book is available from the British Library

ISBN 1-85078-461-2

Cover design by FourNineZero
Typeset by Temple Design
Printed in Great Britain by Bell and Bain Ltd, Glasgow

For my wife, Anna,
without whose love, patience,
support and encouragement
so much of my Christian, business
and professional life
would simply be impossible.

Contents

Preface

This is a book written by a busy person for busy people. I don't know many Christians who don't claim that they are busy. Some feel that they are far too busy to serve God in any way and they are quite happy to leave that to the "professionals" – whoever they may be. But busy doing what? And to what end? And what does all this add up to? As I pose these questions, let me welcome you to my world. It is the real world of someone who is involved daily in all kinds of business and professional matters, with the attendant pressures and problems. I did not write this book in a quiet retreat, but in snatched hours between meetings, in hotels and after long plane journeys. The questions this book poses are ones I regularly ask myself, and every so often I need to step back and really search for answers to such questions. And so this book asks the hard questions and seeks godly, biblical answers. This book reflects my own life's struggle - it is part of the route map of my own journey. Let me assure you that if I had waited until I had time to write it, there would be nothing here for you to read! But here it is. The question at the heart of this book, "Whose life is it anyway?" is one of the most fundamental questions a Christian can ask. In fact, there are few more fundamental. As you read on, try not to shirk from this question, its implications and consequences. So let's explore it with a common spirit, recognizing that we all have a lot to learn about this subject.

Why another book? In the course of giving many talks on practical Christian living, I have been challenged by the extent to which the Christian community is facing the issues behind this question. It has become increasingly evident to me that the problems of time and resources, priorities and purpose are common to all Christians – and not just to business and professional people - especially in Western societies. I cannot claim to have solved these problems in my personal life, but I can claim to have thought through them and prayed about them, and I offer here some of the results of that soul searching.

But there is another reason for this book. Although I have devoted over 30 years to writing academic books and papers about strategy, international business and economic development, I have done little writing for the Christian cause. This fact has increasingly confronted me, not least because others have drawn my attention to my own stewardship of God's resources and have asked me to share my experience with a wider audience. They are, of course, excused from any blame for what I have written! I have implicitly accepted that being "too busy" is not an excuse for not doing it.

Who is it for? This book is for Christians at all ages and stages who find that the pressures on their time make it difficult to worship and serve the Lord as they know they should. The book is as much for the business executive, the professional, the student and the homemaker, as it is for those who are retired, unemployed or disabled. One common feature of modern life (and a frequent topic of contemporary Christian conversation) is the speed with which time passes and the struggle to use it wisely. This book is for everyone who from time to time asks "whose life is it anyway?" – most of us already know the answer in our hearts!

What should you expect to gain from reading this book? My basic assumption is that Christian discipleship requires us to engage all of our personality, energies and resources. We do not, however, always realize that. These pages can of themselves achieve nothing, unless we are willing to be challenged and transformed by God as he enables us to take these truths to heart. It is my sincere prayer that this book will encourage each reader to examine whether Christ is in fact the Lord of their lives, what "giving our lives" to Christ means in our present circumstances and environment, and how to use the Lord's resources under our stewardship.

Sources: The core resource here is the Bible, and the New International Version is used in quotations throughout, unless otherwise stated. The book is full of Bible illustrations, and in reading it you may find it helpful to have a Bible nearby. This is not a theological or technical book, so additional references have been kept to a minimum both within and after each chapter. However, as an avid reader of many kinds of Christian texts, I am indebted to a wide variety of authors who have influenced my thinking. Wherever possible, comments are attributed to them as part of the brief list of references at the end of each chapter. Throughout the book I have also made use of relevant quotations from a variety of people.[i]

My other chief resource is experience – both my own and that of others in similar situations. Many of the issues covered here have been topics of discussion and debate with fellow Christians for many years. I do not refer to any of them by name here, nor are my examples drawn with particular individuals or cases in mind.

Structure: The book is divided into three parts: Relationships; Realities; and Responsibilities. Although these three categories are interconnected, they are helpful in establishing a broad working framework. In Part One, Relationships, Chapter 1 considers God's view of us. It is a kind of diagnostic chapter, designed to get readers thinking about their relationship with him and to ask whether they are prepared to obey God's call to service. Chapter 2 examines another set of relationships - namely those between our Christian lives and the environments in which we live and work. In Part Two, Realities, Chapters 3 to 6 examine God's perspective on some of the central issues in the lives of busy Christians. These include stewardship, work, God's rights to our lives, ambition and success. In Part Three, Responsibilities, Chapters 7 to 10 give readers the opportunity to respond to different aspects of what they have read. These final chapters explore further the call that God makes and the sense of vocation that he expects; the need for personal assessment and review; and the choices that face all of us. Chapter 10 considers the practical implications of all of this for our lives and careers.

Acknowledgments: I am grateful to the many people with whom I have discussed the issues covered in this book. My thanks are also due to several people who have challenged me to turn my mind to Christian writing, not least to Keith Danby and Peter Maiden. My debt to my personal assistant, Irene Hood, remains considerable, for help with this and many other projects over the past decade. Finally, I am most grateful for the advice and assistance from Mark Finnie and the team at Paternoster. In particular, the help from my editor, Tara Smith, has been invaluable.

Neil Hood

January 2002

Endnotes

i These quotations have come from a range of reference works, including: *Gathered Gold*, compiled by John Blanchard (Darlington: Evangelical Press, 1984); *Sifted Silver*, compiled by John Blanchard (Darlington: Evangelical Press, 1995); Edythe Draper, *Quotations for the Christian World* (Wheaton, IL: Tyndale, 1992); F. B. Proctor, *Treasury of Quotations on Religious Subjects* (Grand Rapids, MI: Kregel Publications, 1977); *5000 Quotations for Teachers and Preachers*, compiled by Robert Backhouse (Eastbourne: Kingsway Publications, 1994).

Professor Neil Hood
Biographical Note

Neil Hood, CBE, FRSE, juggles a busy life as an international business strategist, university professor, Christian conference speaker, prolific author on international business and economic development, family man and church elder. He is Professor of Business Policy at the University of Strathclyde, Glasgow, UK, and a director of, or advisor to, a number of major companies including Scottish Power plc, Xansa plc and The Malcolm Group plc. He has advised many governments on economic matters, and is Deputy Chairman of Scottish Enterprise. In 2000 he was honored by Queen Elizabeth for services to business and economic development. His life plan to dedicate his time and skills to Christian ministries is reflected in his chairmanship of Send the Light Ltd., in his involvement with Christian ministries such as Scripture Union and Blythswood Care, and in his busy preaching and teaching schedule. He and his wife, Anna, have two children, Annette (married to Alan) and Cameron (married to Ann), and two grandchildren, Emily and Isla. Neil is not too busy, however, to grow orchids, cheer on the Scottish rugby team, play with his grandchildren ... or pray that *Whose Life is it Anyway?* will challenge you to join him in the joy of Christian service.

PART ONE
RELATIONSHIPS

1
Mirrors, Lifestyle and a Question of Will

"For even the Son of Man did not come to be served, but to serve, and to give his life as a ransom for many." (Mk. 10:45)

Outline These first two chapters examine our relationships with God and with our environment. After an introduction to the book as a whole, the three sections of this chapter encourage us to look at ourselves, the way we live and what we are willing to do for God.

Looking in the mirror
By looking into a mirror we see ourselves physically, by looking into the Bible we see ourselves spiritually. The question all Christians must ask is, "What am I like in God's eyes?"

Christian lifestyle
In this section we look at four aspects of Christian lifestyle: namely attitudes, beliefs, habits and behavior. Together they provide evidence of how we actually live. Our lifestyle also determines the effectiveness of our witness.

The question of my will
It is one thing to see ourselves as God does and to dispassionately view a Christian lifestyle as an ideal way to live, it is quite another to *want* to obey God. So this last section provides a biblical case study and the challenge: "Will I or won't I obey?"

Introduction   Since the heart of this book addresses how we hear and respond to Christ's call to serve him, the best possible place to start is with the above verse from Mark 10. We can all marvel at Jesus' mission, not least because as his followers we are beneficiaries of it. In a world in which measurement is so important, here then is our benchmark and our role model. Yet the pressures and stresses of everyday life dull our resolve to follow Christ's clear call. Many of us perceive that our world requires us to live our lives at an ever-increasing pace. So this book examines the roots of our call. The followers of Jesus Christ have no option but to offer some service to him – regardless of the excuses they proffer, or the personal difficulties they cite. Many of us can readily offer an excuse that is some variation on "I'm too busy because...". Highly trained and competent people often point out the uniqueness of their specific career demands; the uncompromising nature of their work; the peer pressure to perform; the impossibility of setting aside time for daily devotions, and so on. And yet, we are bewildered to find other Christians who face all of these demands and more, but who also continue to serve God in a distinctive way. Is it because they have arrived at a different answer to our central question, "Whose life is it anyway?" As we shall see, it almost certainly is.

Although the details of your life experience and background may be very different from mine, we share a common language and experience when we use words like stress, fatigue, complexity, pressures and tensions to describe our physical state and our response to certain aspects of our current lifestyle. Meanwhile, as followers of Jesus Christ with busy lives, we ask the same questions: "Where is God in all of this?"; "Have I achieved the correct balance in my life?"; "Am I open to God's leading in setting my priorities?"; "Am I doing what God wants me to be doing?" All of these questions lead me back to the more fundamental one: "Whose life is it anyway?" When we are able to answer this question, we will find answers to the others.

Have I achieved the correct balance in my life?

Many Christians either do not ask this key question or do not like the answers that the Bible provides. One of the saddest pastoral situations I've seen in recent years occurred when a young Christian man I knew decided to marry a non-Christian. Unfortunately, the marriage broke down after a few short months. He was deeply broken, and we prayed together. When I asked whether he had ever sought God's guidance concerning this relationship, he responded "No, I never did, because I knew what his answer would be." Our task in these pages is to ask the question and come to terms with the biblical answers we are given.

Looking in the mirror James is one of the most practical and direct writers in the New Testament. He says that listening to God but not obeying him is like looking at your face in the mirror but doing nothing to improve your appearance.[i] In the spirit of this metaphor, consider the cast list of Christian practitioners in Table 1.1. They reflect different "states of being," different attitudes, different responses to the call to service and witness. You might recognize some of them but, more importantly, you might find yourself among them. Can you see yourself in the mirror here?

TABLE 1.1: ATTITUDES TO CHRISTIAN SERVICE
The postponer *"When my career is well established / when my children grow up / when I retire (or whatever), then I will make my mark in Christian service."*
The observer *"I'm amazed at how some people manage to run a home / business / career and still actively serve God. I couldn't possibly do it, I have no spare time or energy."*
The partitioner *"I really have to keep my Christian practice and my business/professional life separate. You have no idea what my environment is like. I know that doesn't sound good, but that's reality."*
The delegater *"My role is to be a financial provider for Christian causes if I can afford it. I know about stewardship, but I am happy to leave the teaching/ pastoring/mentoring/counselling (or whatever) to the professionals."*
The puzzler *"I have wanted to serve the Lord for the past 10/20/30 years, but I have never really found a role anywhere or in anything. I often wonder why."*
The juggler *"Life is hectic; I'm able and willing, but I have a real problem trying to focus. Maybe that's how it will always be."*
The explorer *"Lord, here I am, send me."*

This is far from an exhaustive list. There are clearly many ways in which Christians explain to themselves (and to anybody else who will listen) how they allocate their time and energies; what their priorities are; how they deploy their resources, and so on. Not many of them stand up to the "mirror test" as outlined by James. How, then, will they stand the scrutiny of accountability before God?

John Stott makes a powerful point on this subject. He writes, "In the scriptural sense 'vocation' has a broad and noble connotation – its emphasis is not on the human (what we do) but on the divine (what God has called us to do)."[ii] In seeking the answer to our core question, we recognize both God's general calling to the world at large and his particular calling of us as individuals. We are all unique, with a unique bundle of skills, resources and aptitudes. Unless we realize that we are unique, we may be resistant to letting the Spirit speak to us.

All of us in some way resist hearing what is said to us. And few of us respond well to compulsion or coercion. Some years ago, as part of a mission team in a rural area of Scotland, I was asked to address a service in a local church. Its traditions were stern, the pulpit quite elevated and the atmosphere intimidating – especially for a young preacher in his twenties. The minister was present and, before I was due to preach, he felt it necessary to give a strident warning to the congregation to pay attention and assured them that he would be watching. This was not exactly the best atmosphere in which to bring a message from God, and it was quite a challenge to win back the audience after that introduction. You are under no such pressure to read this book or hear its message. My intention, however, is to give you much to think about and plenty to act upon.

Christian lifestyle   Let's start at the beginning and ask ourselves whether we truly believe that such a distinctive lifestyle exists.

The Bible is full of role models from different backgrounds and cultures who are called to follow God, and whose lifestyles are dramatically changed by the power of the Spirit of God. We think here, for example, of Abraham, Esther, Mary Magdalene and Peter. These role models clearly demonstrate that God expects us to live in a distinctive manner that bears witness to his glory. Yet we live in a society that brings many subtle pressures upon all of us to adopt other lifestyles.

These influences come to us on a daily basis from peer groups, from the media, and from the superabundance of alternative philosophies of life.

As followers of the Lord Jesus, we need to get to the bottom of this concept and apply it where it really counts, and hurts. If we look up "lifestyle" in a standard English dictionary, we find that it can be defined as "the particular attitudes, beliefs, habits or behavior associated with an individual or group."[iii] This definition is both useful and challenging, since it implies that the way in which we as Christians live out these four elements adds up to our "lifestyle" – that which we are and are perceived to be. It also reminds us that we need a health check as we consider our own situation. So let's explore this "no hiding place" territory by examining one or two of the distinctively Christian aspects of each of these four elements of "lifestyle."

Attitudes: We meet and display so many different attitudes every day-so what is the benchmark for our attitudes to be? We often characterize attitudes in terms of being positive or negative, happy or sad, worn out or carefree, friendly or distant, and so on. Clearly it is important that we represent the person of Christ by being well thought of in these visible and practical dimensions. But to determine the standard for Christian lifestyle, we have to go back to the source. Paul provides us with a direct answer to this question of attitude in what is perhaps his greatest and most moving passage about Jesus: "Your attitude should be the same as that of Christ Jesus."[iv] The underlying idea is that both mind and purpose determine our behavior and our relationships.

Your attitude should be the same as that of Christ Jesus

Paul is right when he says that we need renewed minds. In short, our attitudes will be determined by the degree to which we calibrate our minds to that of Christ. We so often miss that basic point. We need God's power to make that possible. We live in an environment that regularly encourages us to have the right attitudes to our family, partners, colleagues, and so on. These are great objectives, but few attain them. And lots of secular training courses try to induce behavioral change and alter attitudes in the workplace. But all such aids can only be second-best. And without God's power, which alone enables us to adopt a servant attitude, we will never have the correct attitudes upon which to found Christian practice. Richard Raines was right to observe; "it does not take a great mind to be a Christian, but it takes all the mind a man has."

Our ambition is a central factor in determining the attitudes that we adopt. Busy people are often asked what it is that drives them, and there are many answers to that – some internal, some external. At the heart of the matter for the individual Christian, however, is this challenge: Am I designing my life for my glory or for God's glory? The apostle John describes a number of Jewish leaders who believed in Christ, but who would not confess him, "for they loved praise from men more than praise from God."[v] These words capture the stark reality of misplaced ambition in the Christian's heart. If I live my life to get the praise of human beings, this will certainly show up in my attitudes. Jesus himself gives the ultimate model for our ambitions as he talks to his Father, "I have brought you glory on earth by completing the work you gave me to do."[vi] Is this my ambition? Are my attitudes to service directed by a sense of having a job to do for God? Or have I deemed myself to be unemployed or underemployed? At any given moment, our homes are full of unfinished jobs, or jobs needing to be done that we've never even started. Is this also true of our lives? And will we need to radically revamp our lifestyle to change the situation? As we leave this section on attitudes, we must ask ourselves honestly: are our ambitions sanctified by God? This is a question to which we will return in Chapter 6.

are our ambitions sanctified by God?

Scripture is full of illustrations of positive and negative attitudes towards God. The positive examples include John the Baptist, with his penetrating and demanding call, "He must become greater; I must become less." Samuel was only a small boy when he gave an adult response to the Lord's call, "Speak, LORD, for you servant is listening." Jesus said of the woman who came to worship and anoint him at Bethany with her expensive alabaster jar, "She has done a beautiful thing to me." A negative attitude towards God can be seen in the desire of James and John for greatness in the kingdom. The rich young ruler showed negative views about abandoning his possessions. Even Elijah, at one critical stage in his ministry when he was under pressure and in fear for his own life, declared that he had had enough.[vii]

Beliefs: Lifestyle is also a matter of beliefs. It's only too easy for Christians to go off on a tangent whenever "belief" is mentioned – confusing core beliefs with various practices and failing to get the basics right. Assent to the constitution of a given church or acceptance of a declaration of beliefs will not in itself result in a productive Christian life. One of the best summaries of the essentials of a true confession of faith I have ever read is in the work of Tom Allen. He suggests that three principles underpin our confession:

1. Attachment to his person
2. Dependence on his work
3. Devotion to his service

We can live much of our lives thinking that we are "our own person." Indeed, our society encourages us to think in these terms. In doing so we face pressures to detach, rather than attach. But we became Christians by committing to follow someone, by allowing our identities to be intimately shaped by and connected with one who is greater than ourselves. With regard to this dependence on God, we have to acknowledge that this aspect of our confession is alien to our independent spirits. Of course we know that we are dependent on Christ in that Christians are justified by faith alone. But does that dependence affect my lifestyle, my career choices, how I spend my time and how I prioritize?

If we are attached to Jesus and dependent upon him, then devotion to his service will come naturally. Serving God is a command, not an option. Whether we like it or not, the Bible assumes that followers serve their master. It assumes that we place our lives on the altar as willing sacrifices. It is fairly obvious, however, that many of God's resources are not on the altar – precisely because people like us do *not* want them to be there.

Serving God is a command, not an option

However we describe and articulate our Christian beliefs, our behavior will directly reflect what we really believe. The key link between what we believe and how we live is our lifestyle. In his distinctive and unequivocal way, A. W. Tozer says that the one who "believes will obey; failure to obey is convincing proof that there is not true faith present." Biblically speaking, you cannot argue with that.

Habits: Lifestyle is also clearly a matter of habit. Football supporters go to matches; jazz enthusiasts attend concerts; web surfers search out fast connections wherever they are, and so on. A habit is a settled tendency or practice, whether good or bad. It is therefore reasonable to ask whether our habits are consistent with a Christian lifestyle. Your immediate inclination might be to agree and cite important habits such as church attendance, regular fellowship with other Christians, reading the Bible and praying daily, and so on. How right you would be. They are all vital habits, but sadly many Christians do not practice them sufficiently for them to qualify as "habits." The Bible explicitly encourages and assumes "best practice" from Christ's followers. The "best practice" concept will be familiar to many, whether they are running a home, nursery class, hospital, professional office, or business. Adherence to the correct standards and rules is important in all of these settings, as well as in many others. But, in addition to the good habits mentioned above, we should look further at some of the basic and neglected elements of Christian "best practice." Let me draw attention to four of these and encourage you to pause and consider the extent to which they characterize your life at present. They are all vital ingredients in an effective relationship with God and need serious practice in order to become habits.

1. Silence and solitude
2. Listening to God
3. Meditation
4. Prayer

> A habit is a settled tendency or practice, whether good or bad

"Am I still reading the same book?" you might ask, "I thought this was a message to the *busy* Christian." Less charitably, you might have silently muttered under your breath, "Get real." "All of those things take time, and I have little enough of that as it is," you might be thinking. Now that you have got that out of your system, it's time to realize that it's Satan's business to make sure that we have no time alone with God. There is no substitute for some silence and solitude to develop our relationship with God. The psalmist instructs us wisely, "Be still, and know that I am God."[viii] In a world dominated by activity, we need to soundproof our hearts and minds. Elijah was among those who discovered that, while he can shout, God does not normally shout to be heard. We have to cultivate enough stillness to hear the still small voice.

How many of us spend long hours with the TV/DVD/stereo/car radio in constant attendance? Many times we do not even notice the noises around us. We have developed the ability to tune out, to be enveloped in noise but not hear. Many of us regularly perform other tasks, some of which require great concentration, in the midst of this incessant noise. But I still wonder if that is necessarily the best way to hear and learn from the Bible. Christians need to respect the uniqueness of the word of God and actually listen to God. Our environment is teeming with words, ideas, and visual impressions. I find that listening to God requires ever more concentration, and consequently I need to consciously separate myself from other distractions. For me, that usually means trying to be alone – somewhere, sometime.

There are many biblical examples illustrating the importance of listening to God. Of these, the contrast between the behavior of Moses and Aaron in the incident of the golden calf is among the most powerful.[ix] While Moses was on the mountain listening to God and receiving the law, Aaron was listening to the people – and in short order he ended up leading them in a dance around the golden calf. How quickly we lose the plot! So the habit of listening to God rather than to people is a vital one to cultivate. Moreover, it is possible that we do listen, but very superficially – not an uncommon problem in domestic life. So we can assume that we have a good general idea of the principles of the Bible, and do not need to pay too much attention to the detail. This can occur, for example, in areas where God has already spoken clearly (as in matters of personal morality such as adultery), but where what he has said is unpalatable to the contemporary listener.

the habit of listening to God rather than to people is a vital one to cultivate

While we may be able to find silence and solitude and practice listening to God, meditation is surely almost a lost art for many busy Christian people. But meditation does have a role to play in influencing our minds and behavior. As I write this book on my laptop, I need to constantly remind myself to save what I have been doing. In some ways, meditation is like that – seeking to retain what has been learned; turning verses, pictures and instructions over in our minds; allowing the Spirit of God to shape our thought processes and, consequently, our behavior. Yes, the psalmist wrote in a different age when he said, "May the words of my mouth and the meditation of my heart be pleasing in your sight, O LORD, my Rock and my Redeemer."ˣ But he was trying to address issues about his lifestyle just as we are. And he was also talking to, and seeking to please, the same God.

Finally, there is the all-important matter of prayer. We cannot fail to notice how Jesus devoted his time to prayer when on earth. It is a vital habit that develops into a healthy pattern, and it is right at the center of "best practice." But making time for prayer is often under threat in busy lives. Ivor Powell points out that Satan is far more anxious to keep us off our knees than he is to keep us off our feet. Our culture encourages us to be self-assured and self-contained in our secular tasks, and prayer goes directly against the grain of a culture of independence. To pray with the fervor God demands, we have to pray with a totally dependent spirit. Perhaps that is one of the reasons why prayer is a habit that characterizes few Christians, or why it only becomes a habit in times of special need – when we have no choice but to depend upon God.

Behavior: The fourth and final component of a lifestyle is behavior. Clearly there are behavioral dimensions to our attitudes, beliefs and habits, but here we are looking behind these to the moral base which underpins our behavior as Christians. Many western societies today practice high levels of tolerance for all types of behavior. And when we talk to others about Christ they often respond passively – that's fine if you want to believe that, as long as it doesn't pose a challenge to others. In our post-Christian climate, many people do not know how Christians behave – and most do not care. That is all the more reason for us to make sure that we know why the Bible asks us to behave as it does. The moral basis for the Bible's standards of behavior is not that of being relatively better or worse by some earthly standard. Instead, God sets behavioral rules and principles; examines motives; and assesses results. This is as true concerning the evidence of the fruit of the Spirit in our lives, as it is regarding charitable giving, teaching the gospel, or being kind to children. We practice our faith in the sight of the all-seeing God. A key difference in a Christian approach to ethics and behavior, therefore, is that the standard of goodness is personal. The source of our goodness is in God's own goodness, and we are only able to aspire to achieving this standard through the power of the Spirit. Being good is, in effect, being like God. We are all regularly confronted, even intimidated, by the behavioral standards set in the Bible. We can only take refuge in the message passed from God to Moses in the desert, when he revealed his character in these terms, "The LORD, the LORD, the compassionate and gracious God, slow to anger, abounding in love and faithfulness, maintaining love to thousands, and forgiving wickedness, rebellion and sin."[xi]

The source of our goodness is in God's own goodness

For the moment, we leave the question of Christian lifestyle. We know that we can only achieve a truly Christian lifestyle by God's grace. There are no excuses for not trying – whether or not we try to live this way should not be conditioned by any excuse relating to business, professional or family life. Having explored only some of the foundational principles by which we are called to live, we readily acknowledge that our present pattern falls far short of best practice. We will return to a number of the issues considered in this section in other parts of the book as we continue to challenge the nature and consistency of our life patterns. These lifestyle disciplines come before all other service. Without such spiritual nourishment, we will surely burn out.

☑ **ACTION:** Consider each of these four dimensions of Christian lifestyle. Which dimension is least Christlike in your pattern of living? Why?

The question of my will: A case study

No, this section is not about your last will and testament. Rather, it's about your willingness to do God's will. It looks at the gulf which often exists between hearing and doing. Looking at a real case study is a great way to learn and apply a truth to our lives. So, to examine this question of will, let's look at the parable Jesus taught about the worker who changed his mind. People often say that if you want something done, ask a busy person. The truth of this lies in the fact that many of us can do more – if we *really* want to. And, at times perversely, we will always manage to do what we want to do – no matter how busy we are. How many chronically busy people do you know with a low golf handicap? It often comes down to a question of choice.

☑ **ACTION:** Read Matthew 21: 28-32

This parable, about a father and two sons, is lucid and directly told. For our purposes, let's look at the parable as a dialogue between Jesus and two of his followers. We will then personalize it – a potential dialogue between Jesus and any of us who claim to be his followers.

SON NUMBER 1: The first thing to note here is that the instruction to serve is founded on an appeal to a relationship – a relationship between father and son. "Son, go and work in the vineyard today." The assumption is that the son serves the father; the father had the right to ask. It was exactly what he expected of a son. Is that not a reasonable assumption for Christ's sons and daughters to make as well? It is also important to note that the instruction from the master was clear, positive and immediate. There was no "perhaps you could fit it in your schedule"; no "have you ever thought of being in my vineyard on occasion?"; no "do you have time to drop by three weeks from Tuesday?" The master was asking for work today.

There was no "perhaps you could fit it in your schedule"

RESPONSE FROM SON NUMBER 1: "I will not." It sounds disrespectful, and there is little doubt that Jesus' audience would have picked up on that point. But at least it was honest. Why this response? What was his problem? He might have had several problems, in fact – all of which could be paralleled in our own experience. Let's speculate a little.

a *Problem with the relationship*: He did not like obeying his father. Michael Griffith has observed that "enthusiasm is easier than obedience." If we are convincing in the former but derelict in the latter, that might indicate problems in our relationship with our heavenly Father.

b *Problem with authority*: He might not have liked being told to do anything. Perhaps he didn't acknowledge his father's authority on this matter. Lots of Christians seem to avoid taking the authority of God's call, and the power and force behind it, seriously.

c *Problem with the voice*: Samuel thought that he was hearing Eli's call, not the Lord's. Similarly Elijah, waiting for the Lord to pass by, found the call not in wind, earthquake or fire, but in a gentle whisper. This son heard a voice, but he refused to obey that voice. We in turn have to ask whether, in the midst of our busy lives, we give enough time to listening to God's voice – or if we are just waiting to hear what we want to hear.

d *Problem with the vineyards*: Could it be that he just did not like working in the vineyards at all, never mind on that particular day? There are plenty of biblical examples of people who did not like the vineyard to which they were sent – Jonah, for example. Sometimes our response to God is conditioned by what he asks us to do. Have you been asked to go to a vineyard you don't like? Or are you waiting for a better offer?

e *Problem with the sense of urgency*: The request was for today, not tomorrow. You may recall times in your Christian experience when service for God seemed much more urgent and important than it does today. I regularly encourage new Christians not to lose their sense of freshness and their awareness of challenges of service. Perhaps some of us need to recapture that enthusiasm.

A change of heart and mind: But then there is a great development. The parable says, "But later …" We have no idea how much later it was when he changed his mind. The good news for us is that it is possible to change our minds in response to God's call. Sometimes that can be painful – people feel exposed, open to criticism, and afraid of embarrassment. Why did he change his mind? Was it the echoing impact of the first call he received from his father? Did he realize just how badly the vineyard needed workers? Or did he simply acknowledge the fact that he had made a mistake? The route to changing our minds towards God's service matters less than the end result. The Lord still loves repentance from his people.

The Lord still loves repentance from his people

SON NUMBER 2: The father's call to this son is based on exactly the same appeal to a relationship, and he gives the same instruction. In this instance, the response was ingratiating, "I will, sir." No hesitation, no second thoughts – his is a contrasting and apparently spontaneous reaction. What music to the father's ears, we might think. But yet the parable says that he did not go. There is a category of Christian people that I call "absolutely people." When asked to be involved in Christian service they are among the first to volunteer, they commit themselves unreservedly to meeting ministry needs, supplying resources or helping to achieve a Christian goal – but they rarely do the work. So what might have been this second son's problem?

a *Problem of synchronizing the mouth and the feet*: To put it more diplomatically, the link between belief and behavior was not well developed. In some Christians it never has been.

b *Problem of delivery*: It is possible that he did not change his mind and that the intention to go to the vineyard was as strong in his mind as it had ever been, but he just did not deliver what he promised. Something got in the way.

c *Problem of honesty and transparency*: The response was right, but the heart might not have been. There are many Christian songs that are hard to sing honestly, and one that comes to mind in this context is, "O Jesus, I have promised to serve you to the end; be thou for ever near me, my master and my friend." It's a good idea to read such hymns before singing them.

d *Problem of sacrifice*: When it came right down to it, perhaps the son was not willing to give other things up in order to make time for working in the vineyard. We know from the Bible that God is not impressed by mere verbal confessions of loyalty.

What's new about my world?

As Christians we recognize the existence of three different worlds: the one around us; the one within us; and the world to come. The second and third worlds are both comforting and assuring – we have the Spirit of the Lord within us, and we hold to great promises for our future. Meanwhile we live in the world around us, and it would be naïve to suggest that it does not influence us in many ways. The first part of this chapter, then, is devoted to this world.

As Christians we are not alone in this world, no matter where we live. The Bible gives us assurance in this area. For example, while encouraging the church at Corinth to stand firm in Christ in difficult circumstances, Paul assured them in these terms. "For no matter how many promises God has made, they are 'Yes' in Christ."[i] Reflect for a moment on the vast number of different settings in which Christians have already been blessed by that statement. It is more than likely that others have already claimed that assurance in exactly the same circumstances as those you are facing. Equally, in writing to the Galatians about the pattern of their lives, Paul develops the idea of walking forward in line, holding to a rule and making progress under the control of another. "Since we live by the Spirit, let us keep in step with the Spirit."[ii] It is, therefore, with passages such as these and many others in our minds, that we look at our changing world. Although these great discipleship passages were delivered to a specific environment, they are neutral of any given environment. They are as much guides for us today as they were to the people on the day they were first written.

> As Christians we are not alone in this world, no matter where we live.

The temptation for some of us, if not for all of us, in rationalizing our response to God's call to service is to argue that the particular environment and situation in which we live is wholly unique, constraining and restrictive. In my experience, those committed to Christian service rarely use that argument. Somehow they manage to cope, while recognizing both the problems and opportunities that they face. Others, however, do use this excuse to justify a lack of time and energy, poor motivation, and, on occasion, complete inactivity. The excuse takes substance in remarks such as, "I have no spare time, my work is all-consuming"; "My boss assumes

Case conclusions: At the end of the parable, Jesus asks his audience to consider who is the true son of the father. The resounding consensus is the first, in spite of his poor start. The key determining factor is his willingness to respond to the father's call and to do his will. Let's carefully file that point for future reference. But before we do, let's just dispel any lingering thought that this simple case study speaks of a different era, is far too simple for our world, or does not address the environment in which we hear the Lord's call to serve in his vineyard. The instruction to get into the vineyard is only one of the basic lessons that we will all need to learn or relearn – there are plenty more to come.

Message 1

1. Think about God's mission and his expectation about yours.

2. Go back to the mirror of Scripture, using the references in this chapter if you have found them helpful. Consider what the Bible shows you about yourself.

3. List the aspects of your attitudes, beliefs, habits and practice that are not consistent with a Christian lifestyle. Pray about them, and encourage others to do the same on your behalf.

4. If you have not already done so, put yourself into the case study and ask God to help you learn the lessons.

5. Take your calendar for the next six months and pray over it. Classify the entries in terms of your priorities and the Lord's. What do you plan to do with the results?

Further reading

Anders, Max, *The Good Life: Living with Meaning in a "Never Enough" World* (Milton Keynes: Word Publishing, 1993).

Hybels, Bill, *Making Life Work: Putting God's Wisdom into Action* (Leicester: IVP, 1998).

Sire, James W., *Discipleship of the Mind: Learning to Love God in the Ways We Think* (Downers Grove, IL; Leicester: IVP, 1990).

Stott, John, *New Issues Facing Christians Today* (London: Marshall Pickering, 1999).

Endnotes

   i Jas. 1: 23-25.

  ii John Stott, *The Contemporary Christian* (Leicester: IVP, 1992).

 iii *Collins English Dictionary.*

 iv Phil. 2:5.

  v Jn. 12:43.

 vi Jn. 17:4.

 vii Jn. 3:30; 1 Sam. 3:9; Mk. 14:6; Mt. 20:20-28; Mt. 19:16-30; 1 Kgs. 19.

viii Ps. 46:10.

 ix Ex. 32.

  x Ps. 19:14.

 xi Ex. 34:6-7.

2
Our Environment:
Challenges, Changes and Constants

"Jesus Christ is the same yesterday and today and for ever."
(Heb. 13:8)

Outline   It is only too obvious that we live in a rapidly changing environment in which changes take many forms and come from many different directions. In this chapter we will ask some pertinent questions about these changes. What do they entail? Can we identify some trends? And what remains constant in terms of God's expectations of our service?

What's new about my world?
Do these changes exempt me from service? Which changes pose material challenges to me?

Issues and trends in our environment
What is happening in business and professional life? And what other generic changes influence me?

Christian constants in a time of change
Here we recall some of the difficult contexts in which biblical charac lived. We look at three practical lessons on constants – on being pa the victory, on being read as a letter from Christ, and on being ask respond to the knock at the door.

total availability from me, and I expect no less from those who work for me"; "This is a macho culture, it's a competition to see who is first at work and last to leave"; "My job situation is so insecure that I just have to work whenever I am asked to, whatever the side effects"; "These are the normal demands of this type of career, there is nothing I can do about it"; "I job share and my employer exploits my commitment, the more so because I am a Christian"; "We both have careers and as a couple we hardly see each other, how can we serve God more?"; "My job is all-consuming, but I will serve God better when I retire"; "You have no idea how difficult this is, I am exhausted by my day job," and so on. All of these, and many more, reflect *real* situations faced by Christians all over the world today. No one should make light of them. At this stage we will take these remarks at face value and offer no criticism or judgment. One way or another, the real life situations behind these comments produce very different offerings of personal service to the Lord. And they produce widely differing answers to the question, "whose life is it anyway?"

☑ **ACTION:** Why don't you test the "sound bites" in this paragraph against your own situation? Have you used any of them? If those examples do not fit, add your own; and then prayerfully assess their validity in terms of your attitude to Christian service.

Let's look now at some of the twenty-first century changes that seem to pose challenges to Christian service. For example, it could be argued that one distinctive aspect of our contemporary environment is the dichotomy between those who do not have any work and those who have too much. The former may have experienced redundancy, unemployment, long-term ill health or early retirement; the latter may be in particularly demanding posts, self-employed, contract workers or in that general category in which work seems to encroach on all other areas of life, effectively crowding them out. Symptoms of the latter include longer working hours, combined with increased workload and greater stress. Ironically, however, the difference between these two groups does not boil down to an idle/busy dichotomy. On the contrary, I have heard many people who are without work say, usually with some humor, that they are far too busy to work in a real job. In the context of Christian service, I have spoken to many people in both categories who struggle about the time they devote to serving the Lord. The pressures may be different, but the problems are remarkably similar. John Stott was right to assert that, "Christian discipleship is a multi-faceted responsibility." In response, many of us would say that it sure feels like it.

Family life is another area in which there have been radical changes over the past two generations.

Family life is another area in which there have been radical changes over the past two generations. Particularly important in this context are later marriage, partners who both have established careers, single parents, higher divorce rates, greater mobility, more business travel, longer commuting time to work, and so on. All of these changes affect Christian families in a number of ways. For example, family time is at a premium and is often seen as a trade-off with other forms of Christian service. This can generate frustration and guilt. In fact, maintaining a good Christian home may be the most appropriate form of service for parents of young children – not least because it can incorporate friends and neighbors in similar circumstances both for care and witness.

Challenges to the Christian family come in many forms – one of the most agonizing I see quite regularly is the devastation caused for middle-aged couples when their children in their teens and twenties stray from the Christian faith. In some cases the parents' disappointment simply destroys their capacity to serve God, and Satan wins two victories – one with their children and one with them. One of the greatest needs in many churches today is support for families of all ages and stages. This area of ministry requires much time, patience and prayer, and probably every one of us could contribute to it in some way.

There are rather serious issues surrounding this topic of change, and we will attempt to tackle a number of them in this chapter. Let's set out our agenda. Firstly, in the light of biblical teaching, is it possible to claim that the twenty-first century has some entirely new challenges for Christians – challenges never faced by earlier generations in the church? And, if so, are we by implication excused from the biblical instructions about serving God? Secondly, if this is true about our environment (and that remains an open question), can God not uniquely equip us to be salt and light in such an environment? As we shall see, God has equipped many others for specific circumstances in the past. And what kind of responsibilities do Christians have independent of their circumstances? Thirdly, with the challenges come new opportunities. Are we able to recognize these opportunities and respond to them with all the additional skills and resources of this modern era? To properly respond to any of this, however, may require new levels of commitment from many of us. Billy Graham was correct when he observed, "Salvation is free, but discipleship costs everything we have."

Issues and trends in our environment It would be quite impossible to attempt to capture every aspect of the environment within which each reader lives. So what I have tried to do is to give examples of the trends of the past two decades or so in two different, but related, environments. I have chosen to concentrate on business and professional life because of my personal familiarity with both, and also because they are likely to strike a chord with many readers, both as participants and as observers. You might want to add other environments to this exercise as you reflect on this topic. We should not hide from these truths, nor should we say that they do not matter to us as Christians. That is not my experience. Indeed, there could be many personal counseling sessions over every entry in these tables. And yet, this is the world in which we have been placed to witness for Christ. Table 2.1 summarizes some of the main issues of change in the business environment.

Business Table 2.1 is obviously a selective list. It does, however, raise many of the issues of the moment that have shaped this environment and look set to continue to shape it. Let's make several observations about the list, noting that several of the items interact with one another. First, many of these changes negatively impact the personal lives of Christians and their work colleagues, and they generate greater pressure to both conform and perform. For example, the "corporate" employee is invariably asked, either directly or by implication, to give his or her life to the company. In some contexts, very high-sounding corporate values and mission statements can lull the unwary into a false sense of security. For many Christians this is a real dilemma – they want to have time and be available for Christian service, but they also want to do a good professional job as part of their witness. Second, some of you probably read this list with

TABLE 2.1: BUSINESS IN THE 21ST CENTURY	
Pressures on costs and productivity	Emergence of the virtual company
Greater demands for flexibility and mobility	Redefining core business and shedding others
Training and retraining more times during the career cycle	Changing nature of "corporate" man or woman
Short-term contract and self-employment	More moral dilemmas and in different cultures
Employment uncertainty	Heightened problems for work/life balance
Growing job scope, removal of middle management	Reduced age of managerial retirement and support staff

a heavy heart and see yourselves as victims of this system. Redundancy; "restructuring"; pressures to retrain yet again; job, home and church change as the company calls for another move to a new location; the fear of the "virtual" company and the virtual job ... these might all be elements of your own experience.

While all of that is true, not all of these experiences actually have a negative effect on the witness of individual Christians. Some people show great resilience in the face of such demands and respond with trust and faith. But such radical changes in general can often leave Christians bewildered as to what and where God's will is for them. But there is another dimension to these changes. For example, many churches and Christian charities have greatly benefited from skilled and experienced people finding that God brings them new and different opportunities for service out of these dark experiences. People who take early retirement or who do part-time or contract work are able to give more of their time and skills to Christian work than when they were in a full-time executive post. Perhaps as a result of unplanned circumstances, they make a greater contribution to Christian service than was ever previously possible.

A further dimension to all of this is that Christians in positions of responsibility sometimes have to implement some of these radical changes in business organizations. Many Christians have lasting scars from managing redundancy and downsizing programs, selling businesses into unknown futures, leading businesses at times when owners were mistreating the workforce, and so on. At their best, some dedicated Christians shine in these settings by their levels of care for people and evident humanity, even when what they are required to do is unpleasant. Sadly, others bring the name of Christ into disrepute by their insensitivity.

Christians in business seem to face increasing numbers of moral dilemmas. This is such a key issue that some Christians strongly believe that no Christian should be involved with business in any form. I do not subscribe to that view. But I do acknowledge that it is sometimes very difficult to stand firm for Christ. It is clear, however, that there are certain situations, in business and elsewhere, in which a Christian has to act when faced with moral issues.

Christians in business seem to face increasing numbers of moral dilemmas.

Daniel's example is a powerful one and gives us some relevant principles.[iii] There is little doubt that Daniel knew the answer to our question about who owned his life. Remember, his environment was a difficult one. He was a captive in a foreign land, removed with the rest of the leaders following the conquest of his homeland. First, Daniel did the best job he could. King Nebuchadnezzar rated him and his colleagues as ten times better than their peers. In other words, they were high quality professionals, first class at their job in a hostile environment where they did not choose to be. Second, when asked to do something wrong (worship an idol), Daniel refused to do it because he knew it was against God's laws. We too, in our context, should know that lying to a customer, cheating the government, ignoring employment laws, and so on, all violate God's laws. Third, Daniel would not do anything against his own conscience – even in the matter of the diet he was offered. This sense of principle is so important in "gray areas," such as giving a good reference to get rid of a bad employee, or not being wholly truthful to a demanding customer when you know that his order is not going to arrive on schedule. Of course, conscience can only be relied upon if we ask God to center our consciences on him. Fourthly, we also have to recognize that God has only given each of us a limited sphere of control and influence where we work. Within that sphere, no matter how large or small it is, we have a Christian role to play.

Applying some of these principles to moral dilemmas may ultimately lead Christians either to change careers or jobs. I have spoken to many Christians with dilemmas which they could not resolve using these principles. In such contexts, good advice is "if in doubt, get out." For people with family and financial responsibilities this is often very difficult, but ultimately it is the right decision.

☑ **ACTION:** If you are in business, or connected to it, stop to examine how these four principles from Daniel's experience could be applied to a moral dilemma which you have faced, or are facing. If you are not involved in business, apply the principles to a dilemma in your own personal context. Then pray for yourself and others in such situations. This is not an easy issue!

Professions   Table 2.2 lists similar issues for professionals such as teachers, civil servants, lawyers, accountants, social workers, doctors, nurses and many others. While some of the environmental changes are the same for them as they are for Christians in businesses, there are also some notable differences. For example, Christians tend to be well represented among public servants, especially in the caring professions. Many of these Christians struggle with the perceived devaluation of the job to which they had a genuine sense of Christian calling. This in turn can lead to a sense of personal disillusion and confusion, which in recent years has been associated with some of the new paradigms mentioned in the table. Behind such ideas are many fine Christians who have much to offer in service areas closely associated with their professional competence. But they find their jobs redefined, their roles reassessed, and their lives so frequently rearranged that they have either very little or no energy left for other activity. Add to this some of the other issues mentioned in Table 2.2 – such as working in process-centered structures where, in addition to daily tasks, employees are engaged in endless committees, working groups and task forces – and it is easy to see why some Christians lose their sense of who they are really working for.

Table 2.2: PROFESSIONS IN THE 21ST CENTURY	
New organizational paradigms (privatization, market testing, outsourcing, value for money, quality, etc.)	Labor supply and demand imbalances
Changes in output measures	Erosion of boundaries between some professions
Compliance and litigation	Deregulation and new entrants
Devaluation of the perceived worth of public services	Process-dominated management

For some, the central issue here is a clash of cultures and philosophies. This clash has sometimes been evident in the caring professions when successive governments have tried to apply business principles in areas such as medical care, hospital management, schools, social work, and so on. Without going into the rights and wrongs of such policies, the result is that some people feel their technical skills are devalued, their professional judgment questioned, and their job environment so radically changed that they question if this is where God wants them to be. I have met many Christians in this category in recent years, as well as some people on "the other side" who are trying to introduce such changes. Either way, many of these changes have disrupted people's personal and professional lives and have therefore had a negative impact on people doing Christian service.

Many Christians have also been asked to subscribe to management and change philosophies, some of which have a strong new age content. Taken to their logical conclusion, some of the theories of self-realization and empowerment challenge the core principles of our faith and deny the dependence on Christ, which is at the center of discipleship. A few years ago I was speaking at a business conference and was introduced by a leading change consultant who was eager to let the audience know about her own mission in life. And so in her opening remarks she modestly summarized her mission by saying, "I transform people." There is much of this spirit about today, and the shelves of business bookstores are full of it. At one level, Christians can smile and pass on. At another level, living with it day by day can be irritating and, on occasion, threatening.

Many of the trends listed in Table 2.2 are redefining the nature and spirit of some of the professions. For example, professional boundaries are in some cases being eroded as accounting and legal practices converge, as banking and retailing vigorously compete, as information technology becomes all-pervasive, and so on. In some ways this is the normal outworking of maturing economies, and by secular standards it is unremarkable. This does not mean that such changes are painless to individuals, including Christians. Among the many consequences are increased pressure on performance and heightened demands for training and retraining. This last point is also relevant in the wider context of change in our society. Graduates and young professionals today might reasonably expect to have to retrain three or four times during their careers, and second and third careers are increasingly common. For Christians, this is both an opportunity and a threat. It is an opportunity because it can open up more scope for witness within different networks over the span of a career. It can be a threat because it can lead to postponing the development of a regular pattern of service for the Lord. We can assume that God understands all of this and can take willing servants through all types of changes and pressures.

☑ **ACTION:** Review Tables 2.1 and 2.2 and reflect on the ways these and related changes have impacted you in your Christian service – whether positively or negatively. If the effects have been negative in any way, reflect on and pray about some biblical solutions.

… and there's more: What we have covered in the preceding few paragraphs is the tip of a very large iceberg. Table 2.3 reminds us that these specific changes are taking place within a broader context of social trends that impact upon Christian witness.

It is critically important that we are not overwhelmed by all of this. None of us can assume that this would all be easier if we were in a different profession, culture or time zone. Neither is it helpful to fabricate a list of "approved" Christian professions and wish that we were in one of them. No such list exists. We should not regard our environment as having a neutral effect on how we behave as Christians. It is far from neutral for most

TABLE 2.3: GENERAL SOCIAL TRENDS AND CHRISTIAN WITNESS	
More leisure, yet more pressure	But a widespread sense of having less time
More interest in physical health and the environment	But less interest in spiritual health
More technological change	New forces for good and evil such as the Internet
More pluralistic society in both culture and religion	Greater need for salt and light behavior
More noise and distractions, more media and communication channels, more information	Less spiritual knowledge
More erosion of the moral base of society, what Francis Schaeffer called "the loss of the Reformation memory"	Yet more evidence of aggressive fundamentalism
More secular society, one effect of which is that many no longer believe in truth established for all time, not even as an ideal	Yet more people searching for something new and unreachable
More tolerance of different belief systems	But any "faith based" belief is acceptable, and often it is more difficult to set out what it means to be a follower of Jesus Christ

of us, and we should not be made to feel less Christian because it does affect us. But we are called to be Christian in all contexts – sometimes we have to grin and bear certain situations, sometimes we need to attempt to change certain circumstances. Paul encourages us to "endure" – to turn problems into a triumph.[iv] The text from Hebrews 13:8 quoted at the beginning of this chapter should encourage us in all of this. We are challenged, comforted and assured in the knowledge that, wherever or whenever we are, the Lord remains the same.

The psalmist was among those who testified to this, "But you remain the same, and your years will never end."[v] C. H. Spurgeon also encourages us in his personal declaration, "Nothing binds me to my Lord like a strong belief in His changeless love." To sustain us and ground these points in our hearts and establish them in our minds, the next section looks at some further biblical teaching about the Christian life – regardless of the environment in which we find ourselves. The emphasis is on identifying time-independent principles that can guide our response to circumstances.

Christian constants in a time of change Although we will not find direct evidence of many of the issues listed in Tables 2.1 and 2.2 in our Bibles, we will find some of them – even in very different societies. For example, Moses was really stressed about his job change when God called him to lead Israel to the promised land. Talk about fast track retraining! The Christians and the Jews did not welcome or encourage Paul when he was called on the Damascus road to a radical career change. He could later say, "let no one cause me trouble, for I bear on my body the marks of Jesus."[vi] And think of the many pressures on Joseph at different times throughout his life, not least in the massive seven-year project to prepare Egypt for the famine. We would struggle to find evidence to support the hypothesis that many of the great biblical heroes had a consistently supportive environment in which to serve God. For our purposes in this section there are two important biblical constants to address.

Moses was really stressed about his job change when God called him to lead Israel to the promised land.

Firstly, all Christians are called to ongoing service; secondly, all Christians have a responsibility to live with integrity as those belonging to Christ – regardless of their business, professional or family setting. There is also a clear expectation of integrity in our secular work that will in and of itself speak of the lordship of Christ – a subject to which we return in Chapter 7. Now we turn to three very practical lessons.

Being part of the victory What are the essential elements of Christian integrity? I suspect that, like me, you have regularly been impressed by the highest levels of uprightness, honesty and professionalism in some people who claim no faith of any kind. This merely redoubles the Christian challenge. The foundations for Christian practice are to be found in the changeless character of God, and not in a set of rules (although rules are also important, as we shall see). The three divine characteristics that are relevant to our behavior and practice are God's holiness, justice and love. We need to make sure that we know the God we are called to serve. This is essential if we are to feel part of the victory that Jesus won, wherever we are. Paul captures this thought in a letter to Corinth, "But thanks be to God, who always leads us in triumphal procession in Christ and through us spreads everywhere the fragrance of the knowledge of him."[vii] This verse tests our commitment. We do not always feel as if we are living our lives in triumph, nor do our lives always exude the correct fragrance. We can sweeten the air in our homes with an aerosol can appropriately labeled "Summer Fragrance," "Apple Blossom," or the equivalent. The names raise expectations of pleasant fragrances designed to dispel the unpleasant smells. Sometimes when we press the button we hear a soft hiss but smell no pleasant aroma. The container is empty, in spite of the promise it still carries on the outside. The essential challenge in our lives is to emit a fragrance of Christ. Sometimes people interact with us and expect to learn something about who God is simply because we claim to belong to Christ. Unfortunately, sometimes the last thing they get from coming into contact with us is a good impression of our Lord.

> We need to make sure that we know the God we are called to serve.

Paul's verse and the metaphor of the victory procession reminds me of a story from my childhood. I remember watching a young man who passed our house every day as he ran to and from his place of employment. He died at a very young age, as the result of a tragic accident. In his memory, his colleagues of all shapes and sizes decided to have an annual race over the exact ten-mile route that he ran each day. My lasting memory of watching this race is the struggle many had to complete the race – yet all wore its insignia, boldly proclaiming that they were taking part in the same race. By the time they reached our house, many were lagging far behind the leader. But they were still following him and determined to complete the course for this good cause. They did this, driven on by the memory of a friend who had died.

I have often thought of this experience in the context of this verse from 2 Corinthians. God needs followers who are committed to run the race and spread the fragrance of Christ wherever they are. Paul's reference is to a literal triumphal procession such as those that take place after a long war. The aim is to include everyone who has been involved in the triumph in any way – from the leaders at the front to those who stayed behind making the weapons, cultivating the fields, caring for the children, and so on. Every Christian is in this procession, and at its head is Christ the Lord. Perhaps there are times when we need to think less about what we regard as the unique circumstances of our environment, and more about the victorious Savior who has gone on ahead of us.

Being read as a letter from Christ

Corinth was not an easy place in which to live as a Christian. It was certainly a great city, but it was also wicked. Indeed, its reputation was for both commercial prosperity and drunken and immoral debauchery. Paul wrote these words to Christians in that environment: "You are a letter from Christ, the result of our ministry, written not with ink but with the Spirit of the living God, not on tablets of stone but on tablets of human hearts."[viii] We all understand the role of letters in business and family life, and so the lessons for us are simple and direct. We are Christian letters proclaiming the good news of Christ, and we deliver these letters many times every day to everyone with whom we come in contact. These letters are from the Spirit, since it is he who has engraved them on the tablets of our hearts. And here is the crucial point in our study. Nobody can live for Christ in any environment, let alone in one that may be hostile, without the power of God. The question is, what kind of letter are you? The following simple questions will help you find out.

We are Christian letters proclaiming the good news of Christ

Is it legible? Many handwritten letters are illegible, so that meanings, facts and the message are often distorted. Sometimes an expert is required to read our writing. The people around us are not experts in reading this letter, so it had better be clear. We need to communicate the message of Christ using language that our audience understands, always reinforcing our words with our actions.

Does the reader know the language? People can see sermons better than they can hear them. We might not even have to use words to convey the love of Christ. Often without even realizing it, Christians use code words that only they understand – biblical references, acronyms, theological references (e.g., justification, sanctification, born again, Spirit-filled, InterVarsity, S.U., Green Belt, etc.).

Is this letter signed? No one likes anonymous letters. The Christian has to fully identify with the message. If this is Christ's letter, and that is Paul's point, it has to reflect the character of its original author.

Does it have content? This letter is never free of content. It contains both good and bad news, and it is as written by Christ with a heart of love. Thomas Aquinas once said, "A man's heart is right when he wills what God wills."

A man's heart is right when he wills what God wills.

Is it marked confidential? No, it never is. Every Christian is an open letter from Christ, open to be read by anyone. This is a challenge indeed. As William Barclay once said, "The honor of the church, the honor of Christ is in the hands of His followers."

Does it require a response? Yes, and it usually gets one – though we might never know what that response is. We all receive official letters that demand action. We sow the Christian seed even though we may not be part of the harvest team.

Here, then, is another picture of the way in which the Lord wishes to use us. It calls all of us to reassess our witness. The Greek philosopher Plato once said that a good teacher does not write his message in ink that fades or in words that cannot speak. Rather, he finds a disciple and sows the seed of the message in a heart that understands, and thus writes his message upon human beings. That is exactly what has happened to each and every Christian, including you and me, although we might have forgotten how.

Responding to the knock at the door John paints one of the most famous New Testament pictures of Christ when he writes to the church in Laodicea. "Here I am! I stand at the door and knock. If anyone hears my voice and opens the door, I will come in and eat with him, and he with me."[ix] This was addressed to a group of Christians in an affluent society. John criticized them for being neither cold nor hot in their commitment to Christ. This tepid group was wealthy, but living in spiritual poverty. As Kenneth Guider puts it in our own times, "Many Christians have enough religion to make them decent, but not enough to make them dynamic." John's letter is an urgent appeal to repentance, and sometimes we need such an appeal to get to the point where we are ready to listen to God and be changed by him. So the Lord is at the door, knocking and speaking. Sometimes people at the door can be intrusive, arriving at an inconvenient time. In many busy homes, it's hard to hear the knock. It's often equally difficult in busy lives. A lot of conversations are held through the door, or standing in the doorway. People knock in different ways – from the gentle knock of the child to the persistent knock of the salesman, anxious to attract attention. The key to our response is to know who is at the door. So it is in this verse.

The Lord declares himself at the outset, "Here I am." He is the only one who has the right to knock at the door of the Christian heart. The question is, do we have a sense of who this Christ on the doorstep is? What he offers is wonderful. He wants to come in and eat. John uses the word for a relaxed evening meal here – Christ does not want to have a snack with us once in a while, or meet occasionally for coffee. Yet that is sometimes all he gets. He wants an ongoing relationship of both quality and permanence. He offers nothing less than his constant presence and power, capable of sustaining us through all kinds of change, and in any environment. Yet we are responsible for opening the door. The classic Holman Hunt portrait of this verse, entitled "The Light of the World," picked up this point and showed no handle on the outside of the door. As has wisely been observed, every man is the lord of the house of his own heart.

Christ does not want to have a snack with us once in a while

Where does all this leave us? It leaves us identifying with many Christians in previous generations who thought that life was difficult for them. Our lives may be uniquely difficult, and if so we can only seek the unique empowerment of the Spirit to help us. We are not exempt from the work and responsibilities of a disciple. We each need to be open to precisely what the Lord expects of us, given all the real constraints we may face. God assures us, "For my yoke is easy and my burden is light,"[x] though at times it may not feel like that. Perhaps our prayer should be that we would understand the reality of that promise in today's world. Then we will be better able to answer our question, "whose life is it anyway?"

Message 2

1. What new opportunities is God opening up in your environment? What progress are you making in accepting these challenges?

2. If you are willing but struggle with precisely what you are gifted to do, try writing down the skills you use daily in your secular employment. Then ask God how some of them (bearing in mind time constraints) could be mobilized for him in a new way.

3. We spend a lot of time in our secular lives identifying and pursuing "best practice." Review your own Christian service with that thought in mind. Then pray over the three lessons in the last section of this chapter.

4. Don't apply to God for exemption from Christian service. You won't get it!

Further reading

Barclay, William, *Ethics in a Permissive Society* (London: Collins, 1971).

Chewning, Richard C., John W. Eby, Shirley J. Roels, *Business through the Eyes of Faith* (Leicester: Apollos, 1990).

Howard, J. Grant, *Balancing Life's Demands: A New Perspective on Priorities* (Portland, OR: Multnomah, 1994).

Sherman, Doug, and William Hendricks, *How to Balance Competing Time Demands: Keeping the Five Most Important Areas of Your Life in Perspective* (Colorado Springs, CO: NavPress, 1989).

Endnotes

  i 2 Cor. 1:20.

 ii Gal. 5:25. You might want to follow this thought up in greater depth by reading J. I. Packer, *Keep in Step with the Spirit* (Leicester: IVP, 1984).

iii Dan. 1.

 iv E.g., 2 Tim. 2:8-10.

  v Ps. 102:27.

 vi Gal. 6:17.

vii 2 Cor. 2:14.

viii 2 Cor. 3:3.

 ix Rev. 3:20.

  x Mt. 11:30.

PART TWO
REALITIES

3
Contracts, Stewardship and the Deployment of God's Resources

"Each one should use whatever gift he has received to serve others, faithfully administering God's grace in its various forms." (1 Pet. 4:10)

Outline   Chapters 3 to 6 examine a number of realities that face all busy Christians. After thinking about our life patterns and the nature of change in our immediate environment, we now turn to ask ourselves a basic question. When I pledged my life to Christ, "What did I sign on for?" In searching for an answer to this question we will consider four related issues.

What does my contract say?
What does my contract with God say? This section first examines the Lord's expectations of his servants, and then looks at our understanding of our role in his plans.

What do I hold in stewardship?
What is it that we hold in stewardship for our Master, pending his return and our giving an account?

The deployment of resources
Remembering that all resources belong to the Lord, we identify routes to both low returns and high returns.

Deploying the Lord's resources
This final section considers stewardship in some detail, challenging us as to whether Jesus is actually making a difference in our attitudes to money and material possessions.

What does my contract say? In an increasingly litigious world, a common question posed by many of us in both our business and domestic affairs is, "What's in the contract?" In the context of employment, legislation in many countries requires a contract between the employer and the employee to ensure that both parties adhere to their responsibilities and obligations. "Surely," you think, "we cannot think of Christian commitment in these terms?" If this metaphor enables us to clarify what the Lord expects of us, why not? We cannot, of course, go into a file and extract the contract we made with God when we started out on the Christian journey. And, if we are honest, many of us did not fully understand what we were agreeing to anyway. The bigger problem for many of us is what we have already learned from God about our obligations to him, but would prefer to forget. In some senses this contract is a "one size fits all" agreement, so let's recall its basic elements.

TABLE 3.1: OUR JOB DESCRIPTION
Job description: servant
Prospects for promotion: plenty of vacancies at all levels in this organization
Location: to be determined
Period of contract: for the whole of your life
Reporting lines: direct to the top, straight through the hierarchy
Benefits package: all the promises of God
Security of employment: indefinite, redundancy not an option
Small print: none, what you get is what you see

This, and much else besides, is what we signed on for – in return for sins forgiven and everlasting blessing. We were asked to give the rest of our lives to Christ. This is our side of the bargain. "Hold on," you say, "salvation is not conditional on my subsequent performance." Mercifully salvation is not conditional, but joy is. So, too, is peace. And there clearly are aspects of our blessing and reward that are conditional. God has an avid interest in how we use his resources. It is not an accident that seventeen out of the thirty-six parables that Jesus taught are about property and stewardship. I can think of no better reason why we, too, should be very concerned about our own stewardship.

What do I hold in stewardship?

Good stewardship is one of the central considerations in answering our "whose life is it anyway?" question. The New Testament word for steward describes someone who administers the property of another. If we are going to respond biblically to this subject, we need to know what is involved. There are at least three components to what we hold in stewardship, and each of them belongs to God. Christians are appointed in the role of administrators or managers over these things.

Natural talents from birth
These are the distinct elements of our personality, skills and aptitudes that constitute the differences and similarities between us.

The truth of the gospel, his indwelling Spirit and the gifts received from God
These things were passed on to us, and we have experienced their impact in our lives.

Possessions acquired during our lifetime
Money and all our material possessions fall into this category, along with all that we have accumulated in terms of skills and experience.

You may not feel comfortable with such a holistic and inclusive list. Many people prefer to confine this concept to material possessions. That is a false line, and it is also sometimes too comfortable a line. Giving money to Christian and charitable causes is necessary but far from sufficient to comply with biblical teaching in this vital area. We deceive ourselves to think otherwise. God is vitally interested in what we do with all of the items on the list above. The reason for this is simple – they are *all* his. While under our stewardship, these things remain under his ownership. This truth comes with profound consequences. As Frank Gabelein has said, "Poor stewardship amounts to nothing less than withholding from the Lord what is His."

Lest we be tempted to claim that there are different kinds of stewards and seek to place ourselves out of the "active" category, we need to consult the biblical evidence. The Bible presents three groups of stewards.

1. Preachers and teachers
"So then, men ought to regard us as servants of Christ and as those entrusted with the secret things of God." (1 Cor. 4:1)

2. Elders and bishops
"... elders ... entrusted with God's work" (Tit. 1:7)

3. All believers
Based on the teaching in 1 Pet. 4:10.

All Christian readers of this book fit in one of these categories. And above all it is the gospel, the good news of Jesus Christ, which is entrusted to stewards. We should all be challenged, therefore, to ask how much of our energy and resources go into spreading the gospel.

Deploying the Lord's resources   All Christians are stewards, and the New Testament gives us many examples of stewards – those who fall down on the job as well as those who are models of best practice. We now turn to these practical issues, searching for principles that could better guide our lives. We begin by looking at the parable of the talents.

☑ **ACTION:** Read Matthew 25:14-30

A careful reading of this passage is an important foundation for understanding the lessons that follow. As we read this parable, which is so relevant for our understanding of stewardship, five important principles emerge.

1. The steward is responsible for gaining a return on all the resources in his charge as allocated by the owner.

2. The relationship is based on the owner's trust of his steward, and on the steward's recognition of the owner's authority.

3. All the stewards are under observation, and each is charged with using all of his or her resources.

4. The stewards do not know when they will be called to account.

5. But the stewards are aware that they will be subject to review when the owner returns.

The owner allocates resources to the steward "according to his ability." Many of you are probably rich in natural ability with a great diversity of resources. All of us have some mix of the three elements of stewardship discussed earlier. The parable takes for granted that these are all invested in some way, although there is no specific instruction about how or where this is to be done. This point is embedded in the parable; and therefore it is also in our contract. Since they are the owner's resources, he applauds efforts to bring him a return on them. The stewards who invest wisely will receive the Master's reward. The "settling of accounts" is central to this parable – it involved openness, transparency and scrutiny in all cases and, where necessary, sanction for poor performance. The steward who hid his talent is an interesting case. Why did he do this? And why was the master so upset? Was the steward afraid of the master, or of trying, or of giving? Perhaps it was all of these, but the fact remains that he treated the owner's talent as a dead thing and buried it. We should be ashamed if we are that kind of a steward. Believers have life because Christ gave us life. What this steward did was no less than a breach of trust. Investment for Christ requires an effort of will and judgment. It has to be a top priority in

Believers have life because Christ gave us life.

our lives, if we believe anything about obedience. Paul Rees makes a powerful point about this, "Stewardship is not the leaving of a tip on God's tablecloth; it is the confession of an unpayable debt at God's Calvary." Sadly, God sometimes only gets the tips.

Let's look at this issue from another perspective. There is both a push and a pull towards us being good stewards. Read below the wonderful words of Psalm 116:12-14.

"How can I repay the LORD for all his goodness to me?
I will lift up the cup of salvation and call on the name of the LORD.
I will fulfill my vows to the LORD in the presence of all his people."

At the center of good stewardship is a response – not to threats of sanction, but to God's grace. This is the essence of these verses. The starting point is "How can I repay?" The driving force behind the answer is a fresh vision of God's goodness. This is equally vital for each of us now as we reflect on these issues. As we see the psalmist making a profound pledge here, it should help us to renew our vows to the Lord in the same way. The psalmist literally takes the cup of salvation in his hands, thus proclaiming for all to see that he knows that God's grace is for him. He then publicly addresses God and commits to fulfill his vows. This is where we need to pause and ask if we have made such a pledge. And, if we have, do we need to renew it on a regular basis? Furthermore, is it publicly known? Most busy people find it difficult to stop and take stock. In fact, excessive and apparently justifiable activity is a real hindrance to good stewardship. I recall how, as a young child, I used to be taken to the home of a very keen gardener who specialized in "sensitive" plants (as he described them to me in a non-technical way). I found great entertainment in touching the leaves, and watching them respond as if by magic. Good stewardship is not a question of entertainment or magic, but it certainly is a response to the Lord's touch. So, in order to be good stewards we need to pause, take stock, and be obedient to God's touch in our lives.

It is evident from the parables, however, that not all respond to the touch or to the Master's instruction. Consequently, there is a well-traveled route to giving him less than he seeks by way of return. Some of the signposts along this route are set out here, founded on Matthew 25 and using business language to make the point.

The road to low returns

Lack of knowledge: of the rights of the owner, of the trust placed in the steward, and of the nature of the review.

Low levels of investment activity: lack of focus on this issue by people who are highly focused on other priorities.

Unbalanced lives: in which the space for Christian service has not been created or has been filled by other activity.

Fear and uncertainty: about the contribution that the steward can make, and about being asked to give an account.

Partitioning talents: using some talents only in professional, business or family life, but not seeking to deploy them for Christian causes.

Ignorance: failure to see that the resources are not ours, but taking possession of them as if they were. We are the manager, God is the owner.

I have been on that road at times, as many of you probably have as well. And I have met many Christians who still travel it. My discussions with them, with a view to offering help and advice, have at times been revealing. Most people know perfectly well which route they are traveling – by self-diagnosis and by the work of the Spirit. Thus there is a group of people who see no remedy to their present poor stewardship. Their time allocations and job aspirations are a given, and not subject to review, reform or resolution. They feel locked into a pattern of life. To put it another way, the Lord's resources are not on the altar. Nor are they seeking the Master's guidance regarding what is expected of them. Still others dispute the type of analysis above, finding it too uncomfortable and direct. A lot of New Testament teaching on this subject, however, is both uncomfortable and direct. There is also a group of people who evidently feel guilty about their overall stewardship (of talents and the gospel as well as of possessions) as defined above. At one extreme, some of them give more money to Christian ministries or engage in acts of mercy almost as a palliative to giving of themselves. Some do radically change their lifestyles, and others even go to work in Christian ministries as a result.

The majority in the middle think and talk change, but only rarely achieve it. All of us need to hear God's clear instruction on this. "Guard what has been entrusted to your care";[i] "Put this money to work ... until I come back";[ii] "... and find out what pleases the Lord."[iii] How encouraging it is to see that there are clear signposts on the road to high returns. And what a joy it is to meet many Christian travelers all around the world journeying on this road.

> ☑ **ACTION:** Consider the signposts of which you are already aware on the road to high returns. If you are on the road to low returns, seek an early exit.

Stewardship and material resources

As we have seen, money and material possessions are only a part of the resources of which we are stewards and in which God is interested. This area cannot be ignored, however, for several reasons. Firstly, it is often our pursuit of material things that diverts us from good stewardship. John Wesley is reported to have said, "Nothing can be more certain than this; daily experience shows the more (money desires) are indulged, the more they increase." Secondly, possessing material resources gives us power and the potential for self-deception. It is amazing how stewardship decisions can be rationalized. To quote J. C. Ryle, "Nothing I am sure has such a tendency to quench the fire of religion as the possession of money." Thirdly and finally, we cannot ignore this area of stewardship because material possessions have great potential for good when placed in God's hands. It is important to begin by remembering, as Tertullian said, "Nothing that is God's is obtainable by money."

Nothing I am sure has such a tendency to quench the fire of religion as the possession of money

The Bible gives us many serious warnings about money. For example, "Whoever loves money never has money enough; whoever loves wealth is never satisfied with his income."[iv] This is but one of many passages that call into question the contemporary received wisdom of "economic man" (or woman) as a driver of our society and its values. One of the foundational assumptions of our Western societies is that we will want to continuously spend and consume, and that we have an innate tendency so to do. It does have to be said that the evidence to support that assumption is pretty compelling. But Christians are cautioned about falling in love with this behavior. Paul counsels Timothy, "For the love of money is a root of all kinds of evil. Some people, eager for money, have wandered from the faith and pierced themselves with many griefs."[v] And again in Hebrews, the following injunction calls for an alternative lifestyle: "Keep your lives free from the love of money and be content with what you have, because God has said, 'Never will I leave you; never will I forsake you.'"[vi] There is little doubt that one of the prerequisites of good stewardship is to be free from the love of money and to be content. We need to ask God to free us from the desire for money and to give us the kind of contentment that can come only from him. Otherwise, our whole attitude to life will be characterized by a destructive restlessness and the call of God to better stewardship is unlikely to get through to us.

The biblical lessons on stewardship and money set out below are designed to be a model against which we can consider our own practice and test our own behavior. It has universal application to us all – no matter how much or how little material wealth we have.

Let's further examine these three activities of earning, possessing and giving. God is certainly concerned with the way in which we earn money. Although he can use resources from any source he chooses, good stewardship is based on the distinctive Christian lifestyle discussed in Chapter 1. We need to have integrity in everything we do. How much we should seek to earn is a related issue, since it has to be viewed in the context of how we use all of our resources, including our time and energies. God does not always get his fair share of the energy we have. You might not want to go just as far as John Wesley did when he said, "Get all you can, save all you can, give all you can," but you can see his point.

Possessing material wealth is another area of vital concern, since Christians are often trapped by their possessions. For Christians, what is considered to

TABLE 3.2: THE GOOD STEWARD'S ROUTE TO BLESSING	
Earning	In a manner worthy of our relationship with God.
Possessing	We hold money only as God directs, subject to His guidance and control.
	We need to constantly heed the biblical warnings concerning the desire for wealth and holding resources for a day of need.
Giving	Regarded as a vital part of Christian service, we should keep the following in mind as we give:
Freely	"Freely you have received, freely give." (Mt. 10:8)
Generously	"…if it is contributing to the needs of others, let him give generously" (Rom. 12:8)
Systematically	"On the first day of every week, each one of you should set aside a sum of money in keeping with his income…" (1 Cor. 16:2)
Modestly	"But when you give to the needy, do not let your left hand know what your right hand is doing, so that your giving may be in secret." (Mt. 6:3-4a)
Joyfully	"Each man should give what he has decided in his heart to give, not reluctantly or under compulsion, for God loves a cheerful giver." (2 Cor. 9:7)
Blessing	God has promised to bless us when we obey him.

be "enough" can never be properly determined by what we see in the world around us or in our peer groups. It can be a life-changing experience for Christians of all ages to minister to socially deprived people in their home country or in a developing country. Such experiences often lead to a lasting recalibration of needs and wants. But many of us may not be able, for various reasons, to participate in such ministry. And so we need to continuously seek God's clear guidance as to what we should possess. I suspect God may not hear prayers on that theme too often from some of us.

The idea of a "simple Christian lifestyle" has been much discussed, and a number of models have been set out to guide both individual and church practice.[vii] We need to look for guidance from the Bible to assess the widely differing views on the extent to which this can and should be done. Plenty of passages encourage us to adopt a moderate lifestyle, but this is clearly a relative term. Paul does, however, give Timothy one demanding standard. Having established that godliness and contentment are great gain, he goes on to say, "But if we have food and clothing, we will be content with that. People who want to get rich fall into temptation and a trap and into many foolish and harmful desires that plunge men into ruin and destruction."[viii] These are strong words, and we should not treat his warning lightly when we evaluate our own position. Turning more specifically to the matter of contentment, the implication in the relevant verses is of a genuine soul satisfaction;[ix] namely with no regrets or resentment about anyone else's possessions. Again, this is a tough standard in a highly acquisitive world, but it is also an essential part of good stewardship.

Materialism among Christians is a curse. John Stott was right when he said that we have been affected by the "spread of materialism and the corresponding loss of any sense of transcendent reality." Materialism ultimately draws us into idol worship, one of the chief enemies of good stewardship. We will not respond to the call of God in our lives if we do not really regard him as God. As the writer of Ecclesiastes wisely cautions us, "To the man who pleases him, God gives wisdom, knowledge and happiness, but to the sinner he gives the task of gathering and storing up wealth to hand it over to the one who pleases God."[x]

Materialism ultimately draws us into idol worship

Having considered God's expectations concerning earning and possessing, we need to think about giving – one of the foundational parts of Christian service. The following practical and prayerful exercise will help us focus on this.

☑ **ACTION:**

1. To what extent does your personal giving reflect the five attitudes in Table 3.2? Systematically work through each one. Do you give freely? Generously? Systematically? Modestly? Joyfully?

2. If you fall short in some of these attitudes (and who doesn't?), identify the biggest challenge facing you in your giving in the light of this chapter as a whole.

3. What are you collecting and storing that limits your giving? And why?

Here we have been looking at nothing less than the life that God has promised to bless. It is the kingdom of God in action today, and in all of this our attitude to wealth is very important. Jesus did not condemn wealth, but he spoke out very strongly against wrong attitudes to it. He told his disciples in no uncertain terms that a preoccupation with possessions was incompatible with the lifestyle of members of the kingdom. What else could he have possibly meant by the words, "You cannot serve both God and Money."?[xi]

The source of the difference: A biblical understanding of this topic is fundamental for answering the question "whose life is it anyway?" The biblical assumption is that Christians should have totally different attitudes to money and materialism than the rest of our world. But many Christians evidently do not. It is sobering to reflect on some of the Old Testament teaching on this subject. When a person had to choose between becoming rich and obeying God's will, that person faced dire consequences if he or she made the wrong choice. For example, Achan hid forbidden gold in his tent and lost his life;[xii] while Saul attempted to keep part of the victory spoil after a battle and lost his throne.[xiii] These are not exactly minor outcomes. And they give us some food for thought.

If the Lord is expecting a difference, where is the power and strength to change going to come from? Our immediate, and accurate, response would be from the power of the Spirit of God in our lives. Few things test a person's spirituality more accurately than the way he or she uses money. The following six dimensions, in which the root of the differences could be seen, are base points at which the Spirit asks us to test our responses.

> **In accountability**
> We no longer answer to ourselves. People in our world answer to no one
> but themselves — at least they think they do. Christians know otherwise.
> Jesus' words are direct and clear, "From everyone who has been given
> much, much will be demanded; and from the one who has been
> entrusted with much, much more will be asked."[xvi]

Having seen the biblical origins of the "difference," the telling question
remains: is this identifiable in my life? And is the continuing work of the
Spirit of God making the difference even greater? Well, you might say, it
depends on who you are comparing me to. It is far too easy to think in terms
of scale or quantity of giving. The issue, as we will see elsewhere in the book
(Chs. 6 and 7), is only partly one of relative scale compared with the level of
entrusted resources. It is much more about the attitude with which we give.
The way we do it matters to God. This being the case, the only meaningful
standard for how to give is Christ the Lord. In his outstanding book on the
cross, John Stott writes a concluding chapter on the pervasive influence of
the cross based on Galatians.[xvii] The area of Christian giving is among these
pervasive spheres for those who belong to the community of the cross. It is
by that awesome standard that we will all be judged.

It is only against this backdrop that we can view biblical instructions about
how much to give. Take, for example, the teaching on tithing. It was a
central part of God's relationship with the people of Israel. It preceded the
Mosaic law by several centuries. God had an expectation that they would
obey this instruction, and that the content of their
personal gifts and offerings to him would be of
the highest quality. The Lord Jesus did not
rescind this principle of giving one tenth of one's
income, nor did he actively advocate it to the
disciples. Perhaps the reason for that is simple –
although it is a good guiding principle, tithing in
itself is not enough to *fully* satisfy the Lord's
demands for good stewardship. The Lord did,
of course, say that the righteousness of his
followers had to exceed that of the Scribes and Pharisees. Paul

*There is clearly
more to tithing
than money*

In ownership

We have seen that the Bible clearly teaches that these resources are on God's balance sheet.

In perspective

The Bible constantly advises us about the brevity of time and the permanence of eternity. We need to get our minds around the fact that we are not in this world forever. Samuel Rutherford expressed this thought in the style of his age when he said, "Build your nest in no tree here ... for the Lord of the forest has condemned the whole wood to be demolished." We should also bear in mind that everything we do is subject to the ultimate test, "... and the fire will test the quality of each man's work."[xiv]

In values

It all comes down to what we regard as valuable. Poor stewardship is effective devaluation of Christ. The twin parables about value in Matthew 13 are so crisp, so profound and so unavoidable. When the man found the treasure, and the merchant the pearl, their priorities and lifestyles were transformed. Poor stewards need nothing less than a new vision of Christ.

In indebtedness

While we might have worries about our finances, Christians are free as far as their sins are concerned. But this calls for a responding love. In that sense a spirit of gratitude undergirds our attitudes.

In mandate

All of us are holding a set of instructions from God. It might be a good idea to ask when you last carefully looked at them. When Jesus sent the twelve disciples he gave them this mandate, "Heal the sick, raise the dead, cleanse those who have leprosy, drive out demons. Freely you have received, freely give."[xv] These last words are riveting, an acid test of our attitudes. As John Blanchard said, "A man in love with this world is not ready for the next one. Materialism is no preparation for judgement or for heaven."

does not mention giving a tenth in his writings, but it is unlikely that he expected anyone to give less than that – especially given his Jewish background. In affluent societies the rule of the tithe can be easily followed in monetary terms, without any of the other resources under stewardship being well managed. Here our earlier study of what we hold in stewardship is fundamental. There is clearly more to tithing than money.

Having said that, the history of the way in which the Christian church has used and misused the principle of tithing over much of its history is nothing short of tragic. Used at times to exploit the poor, deprive the needy, finance the excesses of the clergy, fund grand church buildings and become an ill regarded and inequitable part of state taxation, the tithe sadly lost its luster for centuries. Such practices were a pale imitation of God's original intention, both in design and implementation. In more recent times, many more Christians have adopted this sound and useful guiding principle, which provides them with basic biblical parameters to shape their giving of money to the Lord. There is little doubt that, if it were applied more widely, there would be fewer poorly funded Christian ministries. If we are to answer the question "whose life is it anyway?", we cannot afford to neglect this principle. Yet many Christians do ignore it, often deflecting the force of the appeal by debating at length what it means in practice, whether some income is exempt, whether it applies to capital or revenue, whether it covers pre-tax or post-tax income, or whether it is affordable at all. Is it not better for us to accept the biblical evidence as from the Lord, and focus our attention on what this means, practically speaking, for us in our local currency today? Otherwise we could be as guilty as any Pharisee of fiddling at the edges, becoming mired in the micro detail, and missing the fundamental principle.

Message 3

1. Evaluate your current Christian service against the "job description" set out in Table 3.1. What do you learn from this? And are you in the right spirit to receive it?

2. To what extent are you putting into practice the various elements of stewardship?

3. What are the differences between the road to low returns and the route to high returns? Honestly assess the road on which you are currently traveling.

4. Is Jesus making the intended difference in your attitudes to money and materialism?

5. If you do not apply it already, how do you interpret the principle of tithing in your own giving?

Further reading

Catherwood, Fred, *God's Time, God's Money* (London: Hodder & Stoughton, 1991).

Mann, Adrian, *No Small Change: Money, Christians and the Church* (Norwich: The Canterbury Press, 1992).

Murray, Stuart, *Beyond Tithing* (Carlisle: Paternoster Press, 2000).

Tondeur, Keith, *Your Money and Your Life: Learning How to Handle Money God's Way* (London: Triangle, 1996).

Endnotes

i 1 Tim. 6:20.

ii Lk. 19:13.

iii Eph. 5:10.

iv Eccl. 5:10.

v 1 Tim. 6:10.

vi Heb. 13:5.

vii See, for example, Ronald J. Sider, *Rich Christians in an Age of Hunger: Moving from Affluence to Generosity* (Dallas, TX:Word, 1997); and *Living More Simply: Biblical Principles and Practical Models* (Downers Grove, IL: IVP, 1980).

viii 1 Tim. 6:8-9.

ix See, e.g., Prov. 15:16; Phil. 4:11; Heb. 13:5.

x Eccl. 2:26.

xi Mt. 6:24.

xii Josh. 7.

xiii 1 Sam. 15.

xiv 1 Cor. 3:13.

xv Mt. 10:8.

xvi Lk. 12:48.

xvii John Stott, *The Cross of Christ* (Downers Grove, IL: IVP, 1986).

4
Work: Reconciling God's View and Our View

"So I saw that there is nothing better for a man than to enjoy his work, because that is his lot."
(Eccl. 3: 22)

Outline For most of us, work is one of life's realities. This chapter concerns our work as individuals within our different environments and, in particular, the interaction between our secular work and being a servant of the Lord. The chapter is divided into five main sections.

What is my relationship to work?
We begin by asking this personal question and trying to answer it with honesty.

God's view of work
This section briefly examines the biblical basis for work as a foundation for our study.

God's view of workers
How does God regard work in general and my work in particular?

What's gone wrong?
With all this guidance, how do we explain the imbalance which often characterizes our lives?

Getting things into perspective
This section challenges our own living through two case studies – one on busy businessmen, the other on distracted soldiers.

What is my relationship to work? Let me begin with a confession. I am either one of the best or one of the worst people to be writing about this topic. And I am tempted to hide behind the text from Ecclesiastes 3:22 above. I have long acknowledged that I have several problems concerning my relationship with work. Those problems that I recognize (and there may well be others) stem from several different sources. Because my work stimulates me and brings me a sense of fulfillment, I love much of it. My career has been diverse and varied, and therefore rarely dull. It is too easy, however, for me to fill my days without always taking an overview of the consequences for those I love. My desire to be responsive to the demands of situations which call for added effort can also take up too much of my time and focus. And, in the middle of all of this, it is a difficult balance to maintain a sense of stewardship and to try to be good at whatever has to be done because I profess Christian faith. My secular employment mix in the academic, business and public worlds, together with involvement in Christian ministries, has been a lifelong pattern. Has this always been in good balance? No. Have I always been convinced that my time was well allocated? No. Has my relationship with work always given me a clear conscience before the Lord? No. Indeed, I acknowledge that C. S. Lewis was wholly accurate in his observation, "There can be intemperance in work just as in drink." And we should recall that our God does not want us to make an idol of work. "You shall have no other gods before me"[i] applies to work as much as to anything else.

we should recall that our God does not want us to make an idol of work

I learned two important lessons, however, taught to me early on by two different Christian leaders, for which I remain most grateful. These lessons have undoubtedly played a major role in shaping my relationship with work, and I have tried to apply them to my life, albeit with difficulty at times. From my teenage years, one of these leaders consistently talked to me about people needing to get involved and stay involved in some form of Christian service throughout their lives. He reminded me of the hazards that people often drift into when they do not have such a pattern built into their Christian lives. He also helped me to see how difficult it seemed to be to add on such service to a life pattern once it was established. In the decades that have passed since, I have observed the truth of this advice in the lives of many dozens of busy Christians. Comments such as, "the system I am in takes me over"; "I am on a treadmill with no idea of how to get off"; "the years have flashed past since I promised to serve"; "this life pattern was never my intention"; "I am totally activity oriented (for my company)" are only too common. The second lesson I learned was about establishing another early pattern – for studying the Bible. The lesson was a series of "what ifs": what if you wait until after you graduate to set aside time to do this, or until after your career is established, or until after the family grows up, and so on. The central, and profoundly true, point is that Satan will make sure it never happens. As my counselor said, what we set our hearts on doing, we usually make sure that we do – and if that is to study the Bible, an early good set of study habits is invaluable. He could not have been more correct. You may be a busy Christian; you may not have learned either of these lessons; you may not have come to Christ before many other life-shaping priorities took over. At times only a radical appraisal of our lives will get the balance in better shape.

This penetrating question about work is one that you might prefer to avoid. Like many others, you may be far too busy to think about it. Alternatively, you may consider that as a Christian your relationship to secular work is exactly the same as that of all your peers, and there simply is nothing distinctive to say about the question. You might even want to argue that you are not sure what "work" actually is, since you enjoy it so much. However, on further reflection, you might acknowledge that there are Christian dimensions to work. These include the hours devoted to it relative to other uses of time; the extent to which it can crowd out other priorities; the degree to which we can truly say that our work is undertaken in collaboration with God; the question as to who really is our Master; the way in which our relationship with God actually does or does not integrate into our daily work, and so on. Does it follow, then, that as Christians we can have a right and a wrong relationship with our work? I am convinced that it does. Many of us spend all of our lives wrestling with whether, in the Lord's eyes, our approach to gainful employment is in or out of balance. It is very easy to feel that we are in control of our attitude to work and that it is one of the relationships in our lives that we can actually control. If you feel this is so, look around you – and look within your own heart.

many different types of work can honor God

Another pitfall occurs when Christians appeal to certain Bible texts about work to justify everything they do. For example, "Whether you eat or drink or whatever you do, do it all for the glory of God"[ii] is often cited. We cannot claim that what we do brings this glory unless it is the central motivation of our heart to do so. It is simply impossible to spray paint our attitudes to, and relationships with, our work with some holy white liquid. On the other hand, many different types of work can honor God. Luther put it well when he said, "A diary maid can milk cows to the glory of God."

There is much that could be said about contemporary work trends and behavior as they impact Christians. Summarizing a number of these issues for our particular purpose, Table 4.1 suggests seven aspects of the present dualism that characterizes gainful employment in many societies today. Remember that our interest here is to probe where we stand in handling these different extremes and then ask how this contributes to knowing the answer to our "whose life is it anyway?" question. It does not matter which of the seven dichotomies we face (and some face several at the same time) – they can all produce both short- and long-term amnesia regarding whom we are designed to serve. Even people who are unemployed or unfulfilled in their work can experience this amnesia, because these situations can be associated with feelings of depression and debility. It is improbable that, if you are working, you do not experience some of these effects. We could all design a dream scenario for our daily work. It would always be challenging and fulfilling; we would have consistent confirmation that we were achieving

TABLE 4.1: WORKING WITH THE EXTREMES	
Too much work	Too little work
Too absorbing	Too unfulfilling
Too exhausting	Too undemanding
Too pervasive	Too marginalized
Too committed	Too casual
Too high earnings	Too close to the poverty line
Too qualified	Too unskilled

God's purpose through it; colleagues would be supportive at all times; our bosses would show fine leadership qualities; there would be minimum disruption to our lifestyle; we would be surrounded with people open to the gospel, and so on. Dream on, you say. If you do enjoy such a work situation, thank God and pray for others who don't.

☑ **ACTION:** By self-examination, and with honesty, think through how you would describe your own relationship with work. How has it developed over recent years? What have you learned in this chapter thus far that you can apply to your life? Plot where you sit within the extremes of Table 4.1. Are you comfortable with where you sit? Or is it perhaps time to pray about a job or career change?

God's view of work In order to view our own situation better, we should briefly consider God's perspective on work. From the earliest chapters of the Bible, we see that our God is a worker and that he takes satisfaction from it. Regarding creation, we are told on several occasions that, "God saw all that he had made, and it was very good."[iii] His work starts with creation and moves on to providence, judgment and redemption. Hence the continuity reflected in the Lord's words, "My Father is always at his work to this very day, and I, too, am working."[iv] It is most enlightening to see that our God is portrayed in many different relationships with work. At times God rests from it and is refreshed by it;[v] sometimes he is active in the metaphor of manual labor;[vi] and he also works through delegation to others.[vii] His directing and executive authority are evident in texts such as, "By the word of the LORD were the heavens made."[viii] These and many other passages help us understand the biblical principles concerning work.

What can we conclude from this? God's work is unique, but it is a model for human work. It is characterized by order and creativity; it is designed to benefit others; and he works in a way that reflects his essential nature. God's work is linked with human work from the beginning in that it is part of the

God's work is unique, but it is a model for human work

creation mandate and it expresses the fact that humankind is made in his image. The very nature of work also presumes a divine and human cooperation, a partnership. Hence a passage such as, "May the favor of the Lord our God rest upon us; establish the work of our hands."[ix] Clearly this collaboration can only involve work that is honorable in God's eyes.

There is another side of biblical teaching on work that we should not ignore – namely the sense in which it is seen as a curse.[x] The fall did not bring about work, but it did change its nature. Perhaps we can trace the tough side of work – the struggle to complete it, its complexities, the sense of weariness that we face, to that event. Ecclesiastes speaks powerfully about how work can be a curse when it is not part of a God-centered life. Many of us would say that it is still tough at times, even when we try to put God at the center.

God's view of workers

The Bible sees a dignity in all work, without any concept of a hierarchy of occupations. Work is regarded as a calling, even although we might not always do what we do through a sense of "vocation." We often reserve the language of vocation for selected occupations, whether in Christian or secular work, such as pastors and missionaries, doctors and nurses. But we should not do that. In that sense, a Christian should think twice about saying, "It's only a job." This often implies boredom, lack of prospects, a short-term commitment or something worse. Since work is part of our calling, we need to ask God to either affirm us in our situation, however problematic, or show us an alternative path ahead. If work is to be to God's glory, we have to regard it as an act of worship. Our study of stewardship in Chapter 3 leads us to conclude that all the daily tasks of Christians (whether in or out of work, employed or unemployed) are undertaken as part of our stewardship of resources belonging to the Lord. This is important for our motivation. Paul expresses the point in this way, "'Serve wholeheartedly, as if you were serving the Lord, not men.'"[xi] This is a great text, but it is sometimes hard to remember and even more difficult to apply. A number of biblical texts call us to find satisfaction in our work as coming from the hand of God.[xii] At face value, this calls for thanksgiving from the Christian at work. But God does not always hear that from us.

a Christian should think twice about saying, "It's only a job."

There is a biblical expectation of work, and many are the proverbs giving a dim view of idleness. "The sluggard's craving will be the death of him, because his hands refuse to work"[xiii] is only one example. As to the purpose of our work, the Bible encourages us to earn a living; to express our energies; and to bring glory to God. You will find that work is actually blessed in several passages, so there is no assumption that we should apologize to the Lord because we find our work enjoyable and fulfilling. Psalm 128 begins with such a blessing.

☑ **ACTION:** Pause and read Psalm 128.

We do not work in a vacuum. We work in a social context, often in direct contact with others. As well as providing for personal and family needs, we are encouraged to help others through the fruits of our labors. Paul expressed this as follows, "He who has been stealing must steal no longer, but must work, doing something useful with his own hands, that he may have something to share with those in need."[xiv] The Puritan Richard Baxter saw this in a world very different to ours when he said, "Choose not that (calling) in which you may be most rich or honourable in the world; but that in which you may do most good." Is one of our problems with work today that our work ethic is too individualistic and self-centered? Finally, there are few Christians who can fail to be impressed by the clear New Testament teaching about work to those who lived in slavery. To them, and to us, the apostolic call emphasized the dominance of the role of the Lord in their work. If it could be heard and applied in these hostile settings, how much more with us in what are often relatively favored conditions?

What's gone wrong? In light of all the biblical teaching on the topic of work, we have to ask why we so often go wrong. And is it not the case that we often arrive at the wrong answer to our question "whose life is it anyway?" because we forget to apply these principles to our work? Invariably, when stressed out, overworked Christians come into contact with the Spirit of the Lord, they pause and ask questions like that. Secular work takes such a high proportion of our time and energies during our working lives. In Chapter 2 we identified many changes in our environment but avoided wholly blaming them either for our wrong relationships with our daily work or for our imperfect commitment to the Lord's work through us. The world around us is part of the problem, but the whole answer does not lie there.

What is it that goes wrong in our relationship with work, and why does it so persistently happen? Here is what I see when I look into my own heart at times.

- We work and build careers for our own sakes, without much (or any) reference back to God.

- We forget our allotted time span, and implicitly assume we are here forever. As has wisely been said, life may well be too short to do everything we want to do, but it is long enough to do everything God wants us to do.

- We fail to grasp God's view of work, namely that it is the medium through which we offer ourselves to God. God is God, and he cannot just be one of our projects or future work streams.

- We do not see all aspects of our secular and Christian work as an entity. But God regards it that way – and he looks for both types of work to be an integrated whole. If we separate these, thinking for example that all God asks of me is to be good at my secular work, I am unlikely to bring him the glory he seeks.

- We are seduced by being busy. We often connect success and busyness in our minds. Questions about what we are doing, and why, and to what end, are often of secondary importance. In short, we lose sight of the eternal context to which God has introduced us. Martin Luther once said that he had so much to do that he planned to spend the first three hours of his day in prayer. That would really be shock therapy for most of us.

☑ **ACTION:** We have reached an important point in our journey to discovering "whose life is it anyway?" Try working through the five points in the box above, applying them to your own situation and carefully taking stock of the results. What is God saying to you about this issue? Rejoice if you can honestly say that your relationship with work is healthy and in line with God's expectations of you. You may be able to help and advise others who struggle.

Getting things into perspective Speaking of the importance of the truth of God in the lives of Christians, William Temple, Archbishop of Canterbury in the early part of the twentieth century, commented as follows:

> Christianity is not a drug which suits some complaints and not others. It is either sheer illusion or else it is the truth. But if it is truth, if the universe happens to be constituted in this way, the question is not whether the God of Christianity suits us, but whether we suit Him.

As we have noted, the Bible speaks at length about our topic. The challenge is whether we apply it in a way that "suits" God. One important question to ask is whether he features enough in our plans, and therefore whether we are sufficiently aware of his perspective on our lives. Equally, we are all conscious that while we cannot redeem the past, we can take a different view of the future. God continues to be gracious to the disciple who repents. The challenge is for us to live our lives as an integrated and balanced whole, allowing God to allocate the resources and determine the priorities. In this final section, we will look at two biblical cases , which teach us about taking a different view of planning the future.

☑ **ACTION:** Read James 4:13-17

Case 1: Busy businessmen This is a story about some businessmen planning their future. They were probably Jewish traders. Their language is standard boardroom speak – with forecasts, predictions and plans in abundance. This was a time of founding cities when Jews were often given citizenship and specially welcomed because they brought money, trade and business skills. In short, there were plenty of opportunities, and good reason to be busy. But James makes it clear that there was something missing in their planning.

● *Without providence*: There was no sense of God's overarching purpose in their lives. They made careful and detailed plans about location, time frames, activities, and their clear objective was money. All four dimensions were professionally thought through and vital to their business enterprise, but God had no place in their plans. It was not wrong that they planned – the problem was one of attitude. Christians are not supposed to behave like this, but at times they do. We have a high view of God's providence since he is the sovereign Lord over all and makes covenant promises to us. Yet it is so easy to plan godless futures. Our question is, where is God in the equation for the future?

● *Without understanding*: What did they forget? They forgot that they were human beings, not prophets able to see the future. They forgot that life is short, fragile and transient, but souls are not. They boasted of next year, when in truth they did not know what the next day would bring. Their understanding was flawed in that they acted as if they knew the future and controlled it. How easy it is to plan our work schedule as if we were going to be here forever. James compares our lives to the morning mist, which quickly disappears as the sun comes up. You may recall how your schoolteacher asked you, "Can you tell me the time?", just to check that you could read the school clock or the watch on your wrist. There are times when God asks us whether we know his time frame and remember his plan for us – or whether we are assuming that there is plenty of time to change our plans in line with his. It's possible that we don't understand any of these issues, forgetting the vital importance of using time wisely. John Blanchard observed, "To waste time is to squander a gift from God." He is right, and we all know it.

> *How easy it is to plan our work schedule as if we were going to be here forever*

● *Without God*: God was not in the detail. These men never consulted his will. But James shows them another way, introducing them to life subject to God's will. Sometimes Christians abuse the phrase "if God wills," adding it to a statement as a rather pious sentence filler. In order to have any meaning whatsoever, the words have to actually reflect our attitudes and inner thoughts. After all, it is a solemn recognition that all plans are conditional on the will of God. Of course they are, you say. But busy Christians, tainted at times by the rationality of modern thought, can easily forget this. As Christians, we need to remember that the three-year plan, the next career step, the five-year investment program and all other aspects of our work are subject to his will. The more difficult task is to subject the detail of our personal work lives to God's challenge. But, if we are to please him, we need to do just that.

● *Without humility*: These men exhibit no trace of humility. James, in his characteristically direct style, calls their boasting evil. Why? It is not simply an error of judgment, since it seeks to rob God of his sovereign power. It is often very difficult for professional people to recognize that they are not in control of something. Believe me, I know. I had some major surgery several years ago. In counseling me about the seriousness of the situation, but also about his confidence that he could solve it, my surgeon rightly identified my problem. "The trouble with people like you is that they need to recognize in these situations that they are not in control of events." He was right, although I assured him that I knew someone who was really in control of my life, and that the surgeon was an instrument in the situation. "Humble yourselves, therefore, under God's mighty hand"[xv] is good advice for us in planning our future work.

● *Without obedience*: The Bible assures us that the only way to please God is through obedience. James concludes that, "Anyone, then, who knows the good he ought to do and doesn't do it, sins." These men showed little evidence of any compliance with God's instructions. James calls it what it is. We, in turn, are reminded that withholding service from God is sin.

the only way to please God is through obedience

Case 2: Distracted soldiers

The text for our second case study is from Paul's second letter to Timothy, "No one serving as a soldier gets involved in civilian affairs – he wants to please his commanding officer."[xvi] Much of our discussion above has centered on the boundaries of our necessary involvement in civilian affairs while remaining a soldier for the cause of the cross. The RSV version of this text uses the word "entanglement," which perhaps takes us closer to both Paul's thought process and to our own struggles with work. Our first priority as we reflect on this metaphor is to ask God to show us the difference between the highest standards of professional engagement in our work, and the extent of our entanglement. The means by which soldiers get distracted today are doubtless different than in the past, but the consequences are the same. The following are five examples of entanglement that are radically affecting the Christian community. You will probably be able to add examples of your own.

● *Entanglement by calendar*: Many organizations assume the open-ended availability of management employees. This is seen as part of the obligation of the compliant corporate man or woman. Moreover, calendar schedules are now often handled electronically and are open to interrogation and adjustment by other colleagues. Of course, times can be blocked out for holidays and other activities. But such systems can breed the feeling that the individual is owned by the organization, with visible and invisible sanctions for those who want to live a different lifestyle. This is not something faced exclusively by Christians. Indeed, it is a challenge to the work-life balance as a whole.

● *Entanglement by socialization*: An extension of the entanglement above, here the expectation is that employees will spend extensive time outside work with colleagues, clients and related peer groups. For Christians, some of this is both necessary and desirable – as part of the job commitment and as a means of integrating with the wider community. It is also a vital component of establishing relationships for witness. Once again it is a matter of balance, and this can be both a threat and an opportunity. Taken to extremes, these expectations can be entangling, and a threat to Christian priorities.

● *Entanglement by advancement*: Christians, like everyone else, can fall in love with the process of achievement and its results. It can become an addictive drug that prohibits us from understanding Paul when he says that "Godliness with contentment is great gain."[xvii] Entanglement by advancement takes away both the contentment and the godliness – often at the same time, and sometimes with frightening rapidity.

Christians, like everyone else, can fall in love with the process of achievement and its results

● *Entanglement by stress relief*: Closely associated with all the other forms of entanglement and their contributing factors, this particular entanglement can take many forms. At its best, it presents itself in the perceived need for recreational sport taking up all of one's non-work, non-family time. At its worst, it is evident in the excessive consumption of alcohol, stress-relieving drug use, and so on. There is no doubt that, for many of us, life is more stressful than it once was – and some of that is work related. We have to be very cautious about this form of entrapment, since it has been used effectively by Satan to destroy many Christian soldiers.

● *Entanglement by materialism*: Materialism is a great hazard for every one of us, and Christians are no exception. In fact, some really specialize in it. In a very real sense, materialism can be a cul-de-sac from which escape is almost impossible without turning to go back out the way you came. Its critical and subtle strategy is to reduce our sense of the sovereign power of God. Stephen Alford once expressed it as follows: "Materialism, open or disguised, is the logical result of thinking that above and beyond this world there is nothing else."

However we rate ourselves with regard to these five issues, we will find it hard to deny that they all have the potential to cause displeasure to our spiritual commanding officer. Here, and elsewhere in the Bible, God clearly and consistently communicates his expectation that he wants us to be engaged in battle for him. From this he derives pleasure. Many of us arrive at the battle weary and worn down by many burdens; too busy engaged in collecting booty from this world; and too preoccupied to remember who the real enemy is or how he fights his battles. Meanwhile, the army of the Lord is depleted by our absence from the front line.

> ✔ **ACTION:** Think about the ways in which these two cases reflect your own relationship to work. Avoid the temptation (an easy one for all of us) to conclude that you know several people to whom they apply, but that you are unaffected. This is a superb way of deflecting the Spirit from speaking into your heart.

Message 4

1. Do you have any plans to review your relationship with work? What would it take to achieve that?

2. What can Christians do to develop the sense of community that is associated with work in the Bible?

3. Go back to fundamentals, and ask God to either confirm you in your present work or show you another way ahead.

4. In the light of these first four chapters, assess how relevant your relationship with your secular work is to your personal answer to "whose life is it anyway?"

Further reading

Curran, Peter, *All the Hours God Sends?* (Leicester: IVP, 2000).

Green, Michael, *Freed to Serve: Training and Equipping for Ministry* (Dallas, TX: Word, 2nd edn., 1988).

MacDonald, Gordon, *Ordering Your Private World* (Nashville, TN: Oliver-Nelson, exp. edn., 1985).

Sherman, Doug and William Hendricks, *Your Work Matters to God* (Colorado Springs, CO: NavPress, 1992).

Endnotes

i Ex. 20:3.	vii Jn. 1:3.	xiii Prov. 21:25.
ii 1 Cor. 10:31.	viii Ps. 33:6.	xiv Eph. 4:28.
iii Gen. 1:31.	ix Ps. 90:17.	xv 1 Pet. 5:6.
iv Jn. 5:17.	x Gen. 3:17-19.	xvi 2 Tim. 2:4.
v Ex. 31:7.	xi Eph. 6:7.	xvii 1 Tim. 6:6.
vi Isa. 45:9.	xii E.g., Eccl. 2:24.	

5
Living our Lives:
The Balance between God and Caesar

"Then Jesus said to them, 'Give to Caesar what is Caesar's and to God what is God's.' And they were amazed at him." (Mk. 12:17)

Outline   We turn now to explore another of life's realities, namely the relationships that we have with our various masters and others who have a claim to part of our lives. In particular, we will consider the tensions between earthly demands and the demands of Christ our Lord in the following three sections.

Who has a right to my life?
What does it mean to be a follower of Jesus? It involves recognizing our commitments to him and to others who have a just claim on our time and energies. This section sets out some principles to guide us.

How should I allocate my time?
We all have problems with time – too much or too little. Does God have a maximum and minimum expectation of time from us? Does he control my time? And what is he expecting me to do with it?

God and Caesar: A clash of kingdoms
This section takes an up-to-date look at how we are to give to both the world (Caesar) and to God. The challenging question is, does God get back from us what he deserves?

Who has a right to my life? We now consider another key issue that lies at the center of our attitude to discipleship. In the sense in which we are using this word here, the question is, "who has a just claim to my life?" With others who play various vital roles in our lives, we might immediately answer that there are many such claims. Marriage partners and family; friends and relations; employers and peer groups; and fellow workers in church and other Christian ministries might be among those we cite. As Christians we recognize that all of them are legitimately on our list, and some must be high on that list if we are to fulfill our obligations to God. The claims of all of these people and groups can be strong and sometimes overpowering. If we were to order them according to priority, our rankings would vary – and each of us would probably defend our selection with some passion. We might even assume that the choice of priorities is wholly unconstrained – that it's totally up to us to choose who and what is most important, and that there's no moral constraint on this choice. Where, then, does Jesus Christ fit into this?

To answer that question, we need to consult our textbook. The New Testament most commonly describes someone who follows Jesus Christ not with the word "Christian," but with the term "in Christ" (which is used about four times more often than "Christian"). For example, in one passage Paul comments, "For in him you have been enriched in every way – in all your speaking and in all your knowledge – because our testimony about Christ was confirmed in you."[i] And Jesus says, "I am the vine; you are the branches. If a man remains in me and I in him, he will bear much fruit; apart from me you can do nothing."[ii] The significance of that for us in this context is that it implies a *special* relationship of union and commitment. Put another way, when we follow Christ, there is a mutual pledge – he promises to keep us; we promise to follow him. Let's go back to basics and recall what following Christ involves.

● Counting the cost: Jesus never wanted anyone to follow him until they were sure that they knew what they were doing. Nothing has changed in that regard.

- Making a sacrifice: Jesus clearly taught that following him is a full-time job, in whatever location, situation or phase of our lives. For all of us it primarily involves offering ourselves.

- Carrying a cross: It is not possible to follow the Lord and continue to do what we like. His specific words were, "'If anyone would come after me, he must deny himself and take up his cross and follow me.'"[iii] It may be that these words have been ringing in our ears since the day of our conversion. The challenge is to know these words in our hearts and live them out in our lives.

The power of these points has gripped many Christian writers, including David Watson, who said, "If we were to learn the meaning of real discipleship and actually to become disciples, the church in the West would be transformed and the resultant impact on society would be staggering." In this, and in many other things, our brothers and sisters in the suffering church throughout the world have much to teach us. Surrounded by pressing needs, yet without many of our distractions, they often grasp the essentials far better than those of us in affluent societies. And the power of their prayers and the purity of their faith reveal this focus.

If we stopped here, however, we would not get a full picture of discipleship. It does involve much commitment, but God promises to help those who follow him. He promises, for example, to give his followers the light of life – an illuminated path of life and the associated certainty of purpose. He also promises that they will share his glory.[iv] Not everyone lives in the light of these promises. Indeed, these promises rarely feature on the radar of many busy Christians. Discipleship truths are like the "Muzak" that regularly plagues us in supermarkets and airports. We know it's there, we vaguely recognize the tune, but it is atmospheric rather than life changing. Unlike that music, the call to discipleship was never designed to make us relaxed or comfortable, or to give us a warm feeling inside. Quite the contrary. Unless we reaffirm our original call to follow Christ at regular intervals, we are unlikely to know God's answer to our question. The biblical

the call to discipleship was never designed to make us relaxed or comfortable view of discipleship is not one of formal learning, but rather about having fellowship with the teacher. Expressed another way, it is less about information and much more about inspiration – hence the practice of living with the teacher and carrying on his traditions. In the era before books, disciples were the chief instruments for spreading teaching to others. In our generation we are surrounded with books, and people can read about Christ – but they read our lives more often than either the Bible or the books. As Juan Carlos Ortiz wisely says, "Discipleship is more than getting to know what the teacher knows. It is getting to be what He is."

☑ **ACTION:** Before we return to the question in this section, reflect on the way Jesus talks about following him. If the Spirit led you to really apply this today, what would have to change?

As we reconsider our question "who has a just claim to my life?", we note the seriousness with which Jesus regards this issue: "'If you hold to my teaching, you are really my disciples.'"[v] Although we probably all aspire to being disciples in this sense in our better moments, we do not always succeed. Thus we follow Jesus at a distance much of the time; have less than wholehearted commitment; have a constant underlying fear that we might be asked for more than we are willing to deliver; and are in general a pale shadow of the ideal. We understand that Christ has the first claim on our lives, and that his claim is wholly just. But we need constant help to make sure that our priorities are correct. Perhaps you realize as you read this section that you need to make a radical change. A. W. Tozer makes a vital point about having to relearn our way of living as Christians.

The new Christian is like the man who has learned to drive in a country where the traffic moves on the left side of the road and suddenly finds himself in another country and forced to drive on the right. He must unlearn the old habit and learn a new one and (most serious of all), he must learn in heavy traffic.

I recognize this picture, and it is not just a lesson for new Christians. For busy people the traffic is indeed heavy, the milestones flash past at high speed, and there seems little opportunity to pause and check the road map.

Perhaps *now* is the time. The following is a prayer that I relate to in this situation, which perhaps you might want to use as well.

> Lord, I know that you own me and that you have every right to all of my life. There are many others with claims that are often legitimate and very pressing. While I know that I need to put you first, I have real problems in fulfilling my obligations to both you and them. For this I need more wisdom, a greater consciousness of your direction and more willpower. I know that you can guide me to a solution and to a balanced life. Please give me a fresh understanding of who has a right to my life. And enable me by your Spirit's power to put into practice any lifestyle change that you may show me to be necessary.

How should I allocate my time? Many discussions with busy people about discipleship begin, and often sadly end, with concerns about time. Having first discussed the foundational principles of discipleship, we can now consider how to use our time. Everyone seems to have a problem with time. Some people have too much time alone, are in ill health, retired or unemployed, and time drags. At some stage in life people often claim the opposite – that they have too little time.

We need to consider our allocation of time in order to answer our central "whose life is it anyway?" question. Since we badly need guidance in this area, it is encouraging that the Bible reveals a deep understanding of the problem. Paul counsels the Ephesians, "Be very careful, then, how you live – not as unwise but as wise, making the most of every opportunity, because the days are evil."[vi] The accurate and very practical assumption here is that this issue is always going to require care. Hence our prayer must be for wisdom. What do wise people do? The metaphor is of a prudent merchant buying up opportunities, literally "taking them off the market." All of us have the same number of hours in our day and days in our week. We have to realize that the disciplined use of time is a Christian virtue. The second part of this is to be able to discern the will of God, as Paul makes clear later in this passage. In everyday life, the wills of so many people and organizations shape our time allocation. What role does God's will play in our schedules? How often, if at all, do we consult him? Another aspect of time that the Bible speaks about is its brevity. Among other things it is compared to a passing shadow, grass, mist and a breath.[vii] And so we must ask what we plan to achieve with the rest of our lives, given that we remember whose life it is in the first place.

There are three important questions we need to address in terms of time allocation.

1. *Does God have a minimum or maximum time in mind that we should spend in his service?* Even as we pose the question, we can see its falseness. The assumption at one level is that we live all of our time for his glory. We could not claim to do this unless our whole heart was in it, and few of us could claim that this is the case all of the time. So, to confront this question, let's consider two Old Testament incidents. The first is about David building an altar on the threshing floor of Araunah. He wanted to buy the land, but it was offered to him for free. His response was, "I will not sacrifice to the LORD my God burnt offerings that cost me nothing."[viii] This principle still holds. And there may well be a sacrificial element in our time allocation. But we have to be careful who bears that cost. Many an active Christian worker has wrongly regarded his family as able to bear the brunt of the cost.

We have to determine time allocation at the altar before we can manage all the other demands which are part of our daily living

The second story is about Isaac at Beersheba.[ix] The sequence of his activities is compelling – he first built an altar, and then he pitched his tent. This is the essence of the matter for us. We have to determine time allocation at the altar before we can hope to know how to manage all the other relationships and demands which are part of our daily living. It is, therefore, less a matter of God having a time allocation in his mind that he is keeping secret from us. He does not ask us to second-guess him. But we are asked to start by building an altar. This involves being prepared to sacrifice our time, being willing to adjust our priorities, continuously praying for guidance about the use of time, and so on. I ask you, as I ask myself: do we really believe this?

2. *Where do God's expectations of me lie?* The answer to this links back to what we said in Chapter 3 about stewardship. In each of our lives, the specific application of these principles of stewardship will require a time allocation. It would be dishonest to say otherwise. For example, to fulfill the role of salt and light[x] takes time and energy, dedication and commitment. It can be argued that it is part of our portfolio as a Christian, and that at best it is something that we live and breathe. But, unless I am on the wrong planet, it still takes time. It requires more than a casual chat with people to develop relationships. It takes time to explain our faith to inquirers. It takes time to help those many people around us who are in crisis situations. All of this is part of being salt and light.

3. *Does God have control of my time allocation?* At one level he does, since he gives us every day we have. At another level, however, he leaves that day to us to allocate by our own free will. That is how he made us; that is how he called us. He did not install some spiritual microchip that would govern our every action. Part of the issue of his control is linked to our knowledge of his priorities. I know mine – but do I know his? The disciples clearly did not always understand Jesus' priorities. When young children were brought to him, for example, they thought that Jesus might be wasting his time and wanted the children to go away.[xi] In quite a different setting, as Hezekiah was sick and dying, he asked God to extend his life. God gave him fifteen years more, but Hezekiah did not use the time at all well. In fact, he displeased God in a big way in extra time and failed to deliver on the further time allotted. This is not uncommon. God hears many promises from us in times of ill health and crisis. We promise that if he spares or delivers us, we will give him more of our time. If only we were really open to both knowing about and delivering on his priorities. What are those priorities? They include giving more time to prayer, to witnessing, to caring for people, being more responsive to the direction of the Spirit when he challenges our work patterns, and so on. But this involves surrendering control over our time allocation. And that is tough to do.

☑ **ACTION:** Take time to measure your present time allocation against the demands that the Lord is making. If you feel no such demands, reflect on why that is the case. What would "making the most of every opportunity"[xii] entail for you right now?

☑ **ACTION:** Read Mark 12:13-17

God and Caesar: The theme text for this chapter contains an
A clash of kingdoms almost universally known phrase. It takes us
right to the key issue of our service, which is
ultimately a question of loyalties. To express it like that often hurts, and can
cause offense. Most Christians, however they deploy their time and exercise
their stewardship, would like to stop short of having their basic loyalty to
the Lord questioned. But that's the nub of the matter. A core discipleship
question is, "are you giving God what is right or what is left?" The words of
Andrew Murray should ring in our ears, "We ask how much a man gives;
Christ asks how much he keeps."

To help us understand its implications, we need to think about the context
of Jesus' remark and look at its wider application for us. This is another
vital element in our answer to the "whose life is it anyway?" question.
Historically, the Jews paid the tribute (or poll tax) with a denarius. This silver
coin was specially minted for that purpose (bronze coins with different
emblems were for everyday use). The silver coin was a very contentious
issue for the Jews, and all from the age of sixteen to sixty-five had to pay it.
While having to pay the tax was bad enough, the inscriptions on the coins
made them even angrier. The coins had emblems of Roman emperors on
them, invariably with descriptions of their divinity. This was blasphemy to
the Jews, since they saw it as idolatry. But these coins were critical to the
Romans, since their use effectively delineated the boundaries of their
Empire and the right to tax their varied and geographically dispersed
peoples. So the questions designed to trap Jesus were real. If he supported
the rebellion against paying the tribute, he could have been arrested on a
charge of treason. On the other hand, if he admitted that the Jews were
liable to pay the tax, others might be less open to his teaching. His response
utterly amazed them (the word used for "amazed" being a strong one). Let's
hope it also amazes us.

"Give to Caesar what is Caesar's and to God what is God's." The idea is of
"giving back" something as in the discharging of a debt. Jesus implied here
that he recognized that the people had duties to *both* Caesar and to God,
that they were compatible, and that *both* had to be fully discharged. But

were they duties of the same type, weight, or substance? The debt to Caesar could be settled with a few coins and was a relatively small debt compared to the vast debt his listeners owed to God. Caesar, his cohorts and administrators had only given a little as the occupying force in the land, and much that he gave was not appreciated by the Jews. God had assuredly given them great gifts as a nation, and had offered eternal blessings to those who trusted in him. It did not make sense to compare the debts as if they were equal to one another. There are two spheres of indebtedness here – a lower and a higher one. And there are two masters, but only one of them is the Eternal God who will judge the world in righteousness.

there are two masters, but only one of them is the Eternal God

Before applying this text to our core question and to our busy lives, let me acknowledge that there are many other profound dimensions of this verse that we have not considered. There are, for example, many Christians living in regimes that are wholly hostile to the followers of Jesus Christ, where obeying "Caesar" is impossible at any level. Some of these limits to civic responsibility and obedience to the powers that are in authority, whom Christians are normally taught to respect, might well be captured in Peter's words, "We must obey God rather than men!"[xiii] It is clear that, in the life of the Christian, God has the last word – and not the state.

In the wider application of this verse to our situation, "Caesar" represents our world's demands in all their various dimensions. Some of these are fair and reasonable, others are not; some we see ahead of us, others creep up by stealth; some are not demanding, others consume our lives at times. Right at the center of the "whose life is it anyway?" question is the power and influence of Caesar in his many guises. Let's try to tease this out by posing four questions.

1. *What belongs to Caesar and has to be given back?* There is much in all of our busy lives that is his by right. We hold appointments, commit to obligations of various types, earn and owe taxes, comply with laws and regulations, and so on. There are many pressing items in this category. But they are all transient and they are all measured in Caesar's currency.

Important and compelling though they are, they have little value in God's currency. This does not, of course, relieve us from the obligation to be good private and corporate citizens. Quite the contrary – but it does lead us to pray that we can distinguish between the qualitatively different kind of indebtedness we have to Caesar and to God. The truth is, many of us can't.

2. *What belongs to God and has to be given back?* Most of this book addresses our personal answer to that question. The Bible tells us that we are no less than part of Jesus' inheritance. Jesus Christ is "heir of all things," including you and me. We are part of a people created to worship, but fallen. We are reached, redeemed and sanctified by him, moving on to be glorified. Everything that we are and have belongs to God. When we think in these terms, we cry out to God to deliver us from the excessive demands of Caesar that dull our senses to his call to service.

3. *Is it always clear and obvious to us what belongs to God and to Caesar?* No, it certainly is not. The effect of sin and the work of Satan sear our consciences at times when we should be able to make a clear judgment on these matters. On other occasions, we know only too well which is which but have no inclination to comply. And Caesar is always hungry for more from us. His demands at times come in very contemporary forms by e-mail, text message, fax line and telephone. As a result we hear many of his distracting words more clearly, and feel them more sharply, than we do those of the Lord. The tangible and immediate is the enemy of the spiritual and the eternal. But knowing and not paying is the real challenge for us all. During the extensive, and sometimes violent, political campaign against the payment of the poll tax in the United Kingdom some years ago, one particular slogan of protest received a lot of exposure: "Can pay, won't pay." If this applies to your situation, do something about it.

> *The effect of sin and the work of Satan sear our consciences*

4. *What happens when I give to Caesar and to God?* If you give to Caesar, you might get an acknowledgment or a receipt, but not much more. He has nothing to give us. Giving to God is quite another story. Giving of ourselves triggers eternal machinery to return more to us than we ever gave or than we could ever imagine. Our God is a giving God. He gave us

his Son. We came to him with confession, surrender and trust; we continue to come to him with prayer, worship and witnessing; the result is the completion of God's work in a new creation. The hymn writer Christina Georgina Rossetti has captured it perfectly:

> *What can I give Him, poor as I am?*
> *If I were a shepherd, I would bring a lamb*
> *If I were a wise man, I would do my part*
> *Yet what can I give Him, give my heart*

God wants our heart. God's requests to us are always reasonable. Caesar's often are not. God never asks more than he deserves, and never takes more than he gives. It is in these bountiful terms that the Bible introduces us to God's great cycle of returns: "Give, and it will be given to you. A good measure, pressed down, shaken together and running over, will be poured into your lap."[xiv]

Christians face a battleground at the interface between God's kingdom and Caesar's kingdom. We need to be constantly aware of this, able to see that it is happening and able to recognize the degree to which we can take a position and stand firm within it. It simply is not possible for us to do this in our own strength. The things that motivate our secular lives are too strong and too diverse. And we are creatures of the immediate for much of the time. We have to ask ourselves, therefore, about the extent to which this battle features in our prayer life. Do we seek to be armed against the takeover of our lives by other forces? How much of our time have we already surrendered to Caesar's kingdom, to the detriment of work done for God's kingdom?

☑ **ACTION:** This is a very serious issue for busy and successful Christians. Mentally walk along the battle lines of your life and reassess the interface between what is Caesar's and what is God's.

Hudson Taylor once said, "I used to ask God to help me. Then I asked if I might help Him. I ended up asking Him to do his work through me." In our better moments, that surely is the point to which we would all like the Lord to lead us.

Message 5

1. Describe how you are following Christ right now. It might be helpful to write down any difficulties you are having, and keep them available for prayer and for sharing with others who have faced similar experiences.

2. Look through your schedule for the past month or two and broadly allocate the time you spent for Caesar and that you spent for God.

3. Note that we speak of "spending" time, while the Bible speaks of "buying" time. Do you feel that the Lord has given you any further guidance about his buying, and your giving, more time to him?

4. Reflect on the four questions that we asked about Caesar and God as they relate to your personal experience. What lessons have you learned?

Further reading

Carson, Herbert, *Render Unto Caesar* (Eastbourne: Monarch, 1989).

Bonhoeffer, Dietrich, *The Cost of Discipleship* (London: SCM, 1959).

Greene, Mark, *Thank God It's Monday: Ministry in the Workplace* (London: Scripture Union, 1994).

Rae, Scott and Kenman Wong, *Beyond Integrity* (Grand Rapids, MI: Zondervan, 1996).

Endnotes

i   1 Cor. 1:5-6.

ii   Jn. 15:5.

iii Mk. 8:34.

iv   See, e.g., 1 Jn. 1:7; 1 Pet. 2:9.

v   Jn. 8:31.

vi   Eph. 5:15-16.

vii See, e.g., Ps. 144, Ps. 103, 1 Pet. 1, Job 7.

viii 2 Sam. 24:24.

ix   Gen. 26:25.

x   Mt. 5:13-16.

xi   Lk. 18:15-17.

xii Col. 4:5.

xiii Acts 5:29.

xiv Lk. 6:38.

6
Ambition, Success and a Matter of Honor

"What good is it for a man to gain the whole world, yet forfeit his soul?" (Mk. 8:36)

Outline   As we follow the overarching theme of modern realities for the busy Christian, this chapter asks the personal question, "what are my ambitions and how do I measure success?" These matters are closely linked to giving to God and to Caesar, considered in Chapter 5. After setting the scene, we look to biblical guidance on this vital issue in the following sections.

Ambition
Ambition can have good, bad and ugly sides, and we reflect on all three. Having considered the nature of ambition, we take time here for self-examination in an "ambition health check."

Success
Success is a close relative of ambition, and most of us seek it one way or another. So we pose four searching questions about "success": By whose criteria? At what price? On whose time horizon? Built on what foundation?

A matter of honor
This final section recalls Samuel's words about honoring God and challenges us with a promise and a warning.

The way in   Your first inclination might be to avoid this chapter, thinking it's intended for somebody else. It may sound like a title addressed solely to the under-thirties, the young ambitious set, couples wrestling with twin careers, undergraduates, or those in the formative years of their professional lives. You might feel that you have realized all your ambitions, abandoned them, or never had many to start with. But this chapter is actually for everyone – at every stage. We tend to define ambition as a strong desire for success, achievement, power, money or something else equally compelling. When it is expressed in these terms, it is not unreasonable to ask whether these traits can ever be godly or Christ-like. Is it just a ruse for a Christian to call anything remotely related to this "godly ambition"? It is only too easy to retrofit 'God's plans' around what we wanted to do anyway. William Shakespeare's words echo in our ears, "I charge thee, fling away ambition; By that sin fell the angels. How can man then, the image of his maker, hope to win by it?" Do these words speak to us? Should Christians discard or discipline ambition? Should we sacrifice it or sanctify it? We will address many such questions in this chapter.

Ambition: The good, the bad and the ugly

The good: So much of Paul's writing is rich in inspirational and motivational language. His assumption is that there is an honorable level of ambition both to be Christ-like and to work in his service to good effect. The ambition that is good in his terms is that which is directed to achieve the Lord's ends – quite a different proposition from the way we defined it above. Paul regularly uses athletic metaphors such as pressing on; striving towards goals; running the Christian race. Using an illustration from Grecian contests, he urges us to "run in such a way as to get the prize."[i] This is ambitious stuff, and not exactly a call to be fifth in God's sack race, or to fail to turn up at all for the race meeting or the pre-match training. In other passages, Paul implies a surrendered ambition, "Therefore, I urge you, brothers, in view of God's mercy, to offer your bodies as living sacrifices, holy and pleasing to God – this is your spiritual act of worship."[ii] When we consider the direction his career was heading before his

run in such a way as to get the prize

experience on the Damascus road, we realize that Paul understood this idea very well. On that day some of his Jewish contemporaries might well have thought that they had just lost a serious rival to a doomed cause. One less contender as they fought their way to the top in the Jewish religious hierarchy. Certainly, his peers did not regard his conversion to Christianity as a great career move. But Paul knew otherwise. I wonder if we do?

Most ambitious people I know are restless, not inherently content, and in some cases never quite at peace with themselves. Clearly this is not a state of mind to be commended for a Christian. We often observe that it is because they are being guided by a different star and trying to achieve elusive goals. Marie Antoinette, basking in the vast wealth and opulence of the French court, once observed, "I have everything, but nothing tastes." But equally often we fail to observe that we, too, can be polluted by living in proximity to such people. Worse still, we can become one of them. And yet there is something good that God can harness in that spirit of striving, that restlessness of spirit yearning to become more Christ-like. Not being content to drift along and under-perform for God, we recognize the energy, drive and commitment behind Paul's testimony, "For to me, to live is Christ and to die is gain."[iii]

☑ **ACTION:** Read Paul's new job description in Romans 15:17-22.

But wait – does God not need Christian men and women at the top of their professions; to be leaders in their businesses and communities; to be in the top rank of performance in whatever they do? Of course he does. And how do they get there without being ambitious to some degree? The answer is with great difficulty, and only by the most careful guidance from the Lord and by bringing their ambitions under the Lord's scrutiny. That unique bundle of resources which we all hold under stewardship can be deployed in many ways, including taking some to great heights by society's standards. There is ample biblical evidence of this in men like Daniel, Joseph, Moses and Paul. You could even argue that Moses was less ambitious for himself than God was for him. Moses argued that he was not capable of responding to the call to lead the people of Israel. But God knew he was. The enduring issue is how we channel all that energy and ability of ours – and to what end. In short, ambition can only be good and blessed by God if we bring it to his altar on a regular basis.

ambition can only be good and blessed by God if we bring it to his altar on a regular basis

Oswald Chambers said, "In our natural life our ambitions are our own. In the Christian life we have no aim of our own, and God's aim looks like missing the mark because we are too short sighted to see what He is aiming at."

The bad: There is undoubtedly a bad side of ambition, which many of us witness every day. We see it in people whose sole desires are power, progress and position, in people for whom the concept of work/life balance is only something they once heard about in a training video. These people are often big on organizational values, mission statements and respect for the person. They are often charming and very talented colleagues and ready role models for the next generation of managers who report to them. Just as there are obvious physical hazards in passive smoking, there are also hidden spiritual hazards in breathing this particular air. Yet many of us do breathe it on almost a daily basis. Its negative effects can include the peer group pressure that succeeds in pushing God out of lives that have been already pledged to him. But this sort of ambition presents a powerful challenge to the Christian. For this ambition is so focused that, rather like the gyroscope, it returns to the vertical every time it is deflected from it. Although they are empowered by much stronger forces than the laws of motion, our "ambitions" for God and his kingdom are often much less enduring. All too often we end up off course.

For some, ambition is a form of bondage – a subtle, modern version of slavery from which there seems no escape (often because they have forgotten where they put the key to the exit door). As A. Raine reflected on Christian ambition, "You may get to the very top of the ladder, and then find that it has not been leaning against the right wall." Think about performing a health check on the ladder, the wall and the climber as you read this section. You might find you do it in a more honest way if you are on your knees.

On a lighter note, here is the epitaph of an ambitious man from the *Faber Book of Epigrams and Epitaphs*:

A glassblower lies here at rest
Who one day burst his noble chest
While trying, in a fit of malice,
To blow a second Crystal Palace

... a risky business, this ambition!

... and the ugly: Ambition can have its truly ugly side. We associate this with ruthless and self-seeking people who will tolerate no barriers to the achievement of their own ends. History is full of such people, and modern life has its fair share of them. From its earliest pages the Bible, too, has many examples of the ugliness of ambition. Thus the ambitious builders of Babel's tower set out to "make a name for ourselves,"[iv] with little attention to God; while several of Israel's kings seized power in a wholly ruthless manner for their own ends. Several times David wanted what was not his to have, but took it anyway. So, in turn, Absalom tried to usurp David in many a shameful incident.

One of the most telling ugly events in the Bible involves the naked aspirations of James and John. "Teacher, we want you to do for us whatever we ask." Jesus asked what this was and they replied, "Let one of us sit at your right [hand] and the other at your left in your glory."[v] Jesus has just spoken about his death. The setting is solemn and tense. What a tasteless sense of timing they showed by raising this matter. But how preoccupying ambition can be, both then and now. And how revealing this incident was in terms of where their hearts and minds *really* were at this crucial time. They were near Jesus physically, but their self-seeking thoughts flourished in the shadow of his self-sacrifice. Their search was for a throne and for the attendant power. They were more interested in security than in suffering with their Lord.

A distant picture, you say – from another time, and quite shocking. Yes, but we still make regular choices in both the formulation and the pursuit of our ambitions. This incident is one of the classic New Testament challenges to the question: "Do I have the right model of greatness in my life?" Thomas à Kempis expressed it well when he said, "He is genuinely great who considers himself small and cares nothing about high honours." Jesus draws on this incident with James and John to spell out the differences between the power seekers of the day and his disciples – "not so with you," he stresses. In this regard, nothing has changed. God is still looking for a distinctive lifestyle with distinctive ambitions, even though we are living out our Christian experience in another age. In this regard, Jeremiah's words are ever powerful, "Should you then seek great things for yourself? Seek them not."[vi]

☑ **ACTION:** An ambition health check

Having explored some different dimensions of ambition, both desirable and undesirable, let's reflect on how we will apply this in our own lives (rather than judging others who spring to mind here). Try honestly and prayerfully to answer the following questions. Avoid partitioning your "secular" and your "spiritual" ambitions – an approach that is neither tenable nor biblical.

- What is my ambition?
- Where did it come from?
- At what cost am I pursuing it?
- How am I achieving it?
- To what extent is it sanctified?

But the health warnings lie not only in personal assessment. In the paragraphs above, we have been drawing parallels between the Christian approach to ambition and that of others who do not share such convictions. When we turn more specifically to ambition in Christian service, it is sad to note some aspects of the experience of the early Christian church. We need to learn from them. Five of the seven New Testament references to ambition are described as "selfish." "Envy and selfish ambition"[vii] and "fits of rage, selfish ambition"[viii] are but two of them. In Philippians, ambition is used to describe both the wrong motive for preaching and the wrong spirit in which to live. And so we are reminded that the wrong kind of ambition can feature at the heart of the Christian church and even in the midst of Christian service. It is a distinctive selfish ambition which has no real conception of service and whose only aims are profit and power. This did not die in the early days of the Christian church. It can still wreck churches. It is a warning that we should all examine our motives – closely and frequently.

Fortunately, there is ample biblical evidence of a higher kind of ambition. Jesus' declared purpose was at all times to do the will of the Father; while a converted and wholly refocused Paul declares, "It has always been my ambition to preach the gospel where Christ was not known."[ix] At the beginning of Chapter 1 we focused on Jesus' words, "For even the Son of Man did not come to be served, but to serve, and to give his life as a ransom for many."[x] The crux of the matter lies in both serving and giving, and it is clear that God wants us to build these qualities into our lives. The biblical teaching on this subject gives no other options. We need to behave in a way that, to use Max Lucado's phrase, will earn "the applause of heaven."[xi]

Success: Four criteria

Now we turn to one of ambition's closest relatives. Success is often seen as the outcome of ambition, or the degree to which it is realized. Like ambition, the subject of success is a tough one for Christians. Interestingly, a commentator on a radio program recently said, "We live in a society designed to create desires, but never fulfill them." Many people in the world around us measure success in ways that we know in our hearts to be superficial, illusory and transient.[xii] Christians also know that real success is profound, substantial and lasting – but not necessarily recognized in our own lifetimes. Nor is it defined in terms used by our contemporaries. But are we not in reality only too keen to enjoy earthly success in our lifetime? Are we being entirely truthful when we strive for success by the standards of our world and claim that we are doing so for God's glory? It's easy to be pious and less easy to be honest, even with ourselves, in all of this.

the subject of success is a tough one for Christians

This topic, like many in this book, is most productively explored at a personal level. To this end, the following challenging questions about success are addressed to all of us.

Success: By whose criteria? It is fascinating to note the plethora of awards for professional and personal achievements that have sprung up in all areas of life in recent decades. These have been stimulated by the mantra of recognition and the celebration of achievement, and by the desire to inspire people to get the best out of themselves. The phenomenon is evident on a global scale. In some cultures, walls of offices and homes are covered with citations and certificates, and cupboards are filled with commemorative insignia. In principle these can be good things, and I believe in giving people appropriate recognition by awards and foster its practice. It can be an excellent way of encouraging people. It can also, however, be trivialized and deceptive. Sensible Christian people keep all of this in perspective and avoid taking it too seriously. And in our better moments we endorse the powerful words of Mother Theresa, "God has not called me to be successful, but He has called me to be faithful."

We need to consider the measures we use to determine our success – are they those of our earthly peer groups or those of our heavenly master? The truth is, we use both. On occasion we might justify doing so by claiming that the one is short-term, and the other long-term. We might even assert that we know the difference between these and can handle them. It is, however, just possible that the earthly measures are the ones we seek and about which we receive most feedback. The only antidote to that is to check God's standards more often. To do that we need to read and actually use the maker's manual. My son, Cameron, is something of a computer expert. Being significantly less expert, I regularly call him for help. After the usual family pleasantries, and especially if the call is late at night, he will assume that I have a computer problem before I ever get around to mentioning it. He is usually right. And his first question is always, "Have you read the manual?" My standard response is, "No, that's why I'm calling you." The serious point is that it is often more appealing to take earthly advice without going back to the source. Reading the manual can be boring.

> *We need to consider the measures we use to determine our success*

There is little need to speculate about God's scale of values in measuring success. Jesus said, "If one of you wants to be great, he must be the servant of the rest; and if one of you wants to be first, he must be the slave of all."[xiii] I would suggest that a Christian, however preoccupied with his or her career, could never read that and conclude that God had an open mind as to whether or not we served him. One of the reasons we need to continuously read the Bible is that such teaching is radical and totally contrary to our world. We will not hear it elsewhere. And it is too easy to forget it. After all, we know that the ultimate accolade for the Christian is, "Well done, good and faithful servant!"[xiv] Many people measure success by the achievement of their personal objectives. For the Christian this is just not enough, unless we are sure that these objectives are closely aligned with God's purpose. Fulfilling the purpose for which God designed us might not lead to success as determined by the world's yardsticks. Jesus' life on earth clearly testifies to that truth. As Oswald Chambers observed, "Sum up the life of Christ by any other standards than God's and it is an anticlimax of failure." Our Christian sense of vocation will determine the criteria by which we measure our success. This is a critical point, and one that we will examine further in Chapter 7. Without a sense of God's personal calling, we are likely to apply the wrong criteria to our life and be susceptible to others who advise us that we are highly successful by their standards. To them, we have to learn to say "Thanks, but no thanks!"

Without a sense of God's personal calling, we are likely to apply the wrong criteria to our life

Success: At what price? Aldous Huxley once observed that success demands strange sacrifices from those who worship her. Success is one of today's idols, and a price is demanded from those who worship her. The achievement of success demands focus and dedication, and its pursuit often becomes embedded in our lives. We can all cite examples of relatives, friends and colleagues in whom we see the extreme costs of success. Family breakdown, excessive stress, ill health, addictions, ruthless treatment of others, rampant materialism can all be among the symptoms of this disease. But we should be cautious here in making judgments. While I know many very wealthy business and professional people, not all of them have achieved their success without balance in their lives. Some are among the most family-oriented people I know, and many are very generous to charitable causes and good citizens in all regards. Some have a much better work/life balance than many Christians. They make no claim to Christian faith, talk about being self-made, and accept that they may have on occasion paid too high a price in terms of canceled holidays, long hours, missed school plays, and so on. The Christian faces all of that, but also has an obligation to serve God. A minimum contribution to Christian service can be a cost which some are not prepared to incur, simply because it has never been built into the model of their life. Sometimes everything else is there, but the space for service has never been created because there has always been a higher imperative.

"Try not to become a man of success but rather try to become a man of value," said Albert Einstein. This comment takes us in the right direction. But it stops short of taking us the whole way. The ultimate value challenge is to reflect on a wholly different measure, the currency of blood. John, introducing us to the new eternal song, tells us of one who was worthy because "with your blood you purchased men for God from every tribe and language and people and nation."[xv] Against that backdrop, what price success? How does earthly success compare to this currency, which never loses its value; for which there is no substitute; which knows no national boundaries; and whose purchasing power is unassailable? This currency buys souls. Those purchased by it are supposed to know its value and determine life's priorities accordingly. Paul reminds us that we are bought with a price and are not our own.[xvi] Yet we can feel more independent than we should, and it's Satan's business to keep us that way – not counting the cost, never pausing to ask, "whose life is it anyway?"

Success: On whose time horizon? For many in our world, the time frame for success is self-defining – it is a matter of the immediate and the tangible. What can I achieve in my lifetime? When is my next promotion? What if I do not "make it" by the time I am thirty-five? These are some of the common cries of our peers. While it is true that Christian success can only be achieved within a lifetime, it is designed to be assessed over a much different time frame. We know that real success is not a matter of transient fame, but of eternal glory. John makes telling comments on this point and gets to the root of the matter when he observes, "The world and its desires pass away, but the man who does the will of God lives forever."[xvii] The difference between knowing this and living it is often rather stark. The imperatives to achieve often override the eternal vision in the best of us.

We know that real success is not a matter of transient fame, but of eternal glory

Thus we need to consider the time horizon we are using as a benchmark. We can relate to George Bernard Shaw's remark that when he was young he observed that nine out of every ten things he did were failures, so he simply did ten times more work. In Chapter 4 we recognized the compulsion to work from which some of us suffer. But there is plenty of evidence among Christians that work can be addictive and a substitute for service. It can make people feel that the time horizons to achieve are even shorter and can generate ever more pressure. So what does it take to break that cycle and get into the correct time frame? The only known antidotes for the Christian are the word of God and the Holy Spirit. Jesus told the story of the rich fool – a man big in plans, construction, storage strategies, and the management of future cash flows for retirement, but really small in his vision of God's riches.[xviii] He lost the plot on time horizons in the middle of all his planning.

Success: Built on what foundation? Biographies and autobiographies of successful people devote much time to establishing the nature of the soil within which "greatness" was cultivated. Home, family, education, environment, good advice, lucky breaks are all among the trace elements in that soil. So, too, are the choices the individuals made and the opportunities they grasped. There is nothing wrong with any of this, we may well say, and we could all tell our own story in these terms. Christian success, of course, has other foundations in our faith and commitment to Christ. We often sing that we are "Founded on the rock which cannot move." The foundations of buildings are usually taken for granted until a crack appears. Only then are they subject to rigorous inspection and regular monitoring. There's a moral here – and a call to check our own foundations and what motivates us.

There are lots of biblical references to good foundations for Christian success. For example, Samuel could say of David, "In everything he did he had great success, because the LORD was with him."[xix] In a similar vein, when building the walls of Jerusalem, Nehemiah could claim, "'The God of heaven will give us success. We his servants will start rebuilding.'"[xx] Ample evidence of the blessings that come through having the right foundations in our lives is to be found in the prayer of Jabez.[xxi] We need the sense of dependence that is implicit in these verses, knowing that we cannot found real success on the world's civil engineering.

However, the Bible is as interested in the center of our lives as it is in our foundations, because they are evidently closely linked. Here a passage like 1 Peter 3:15 is a real help and a powerful challenge, "But in your hearts set *the Bible is as interested in the center of our lives as it is in our foundations*

apart Christ as Lord." From this moving piece of persecution literature comes a message directed to our hearts, which the Bible sees as the religious center of the person. What, then, is going on at our center? What God-substitutes are preoccupying us? Have you actually inspected the center of your life recently? Your work schedule will give you a fairly good idea where it is. So, too, will a mind scan as to where your thoughts rest most of the time.

There is no doubt where the center of God's affections lies, and who is at the center of his plans. Says Paul, "... all human history shall be consummated in Christ."[xxii] So, then, we are called to hold him in reverence, to be consecrated to him, to set him apart as Lord. This brings us back to the foundation of every Christian life – namely the extent to which Jesus Christ is in fact Lord. This topic is so central to our "whose life is it anyway" question that it is the subject of Chapter 7.

☑ **ACTION:** Consider and pray over that most foundational truth about ambition and success from the beatitudes, "But seek first his kingdom and his righteousness, and all these things will be given to you as well" (Mt. 6:33). How does your present life pattern compare to this ideal?

A matter of honor: Promise and warning

We conclude with a promise, but it also comes with a warning. Our text for this section is one that brings Christian ambition and success into very sharp focus. I have long wrestled with its implications for my own life. It's Samuel's prophecy against the house of Eli, with all its wider applications for us. To this priestly household which had been disobedient to their vows and obligations to the Lord, his message from God was "Those who honor me I will honor, but those who despise me will be disdained."[xxiii]

We all like to be recognized, no matter who we are. The child by name, the lady by flowers on her birthday, the business man by an award, the mother with a thank you for a fine meal, all of us by a smile in the street of our home town. But not everybody who recognizes us actually knows us. And one of the great challenges in life is trying to get to know lots of people. Some people are superb at this, and in a few minutes of conversation they seem to have formed a relationship based on skillful discovery, almost without us noticing it. Ernest Hemingway once said that he never met a man and spent an hour with him where he couldn't have written his biography! How's that for powers of observation ... and possibly a bit of exaggeration! But it is humbling to think that in the course of normal living we often invest much more time getting to know people than we do getting to know God. Society worships, lionizes, and idolizes certain people. We have observed already in this chapter that many of the earthbound role models we encounter can shape our thinking on ambition and success. But what about getting to know God? You might say it is taken as read as a Christian practice. Sadly we know that cannot be taken for granted. J. I. Packer's words strike home here, "the spirit of our modern age spawns great thoughts of man and leaves room for only very small thoughts of God."

In this context then we turn to this passage, checking the very basics of a life of Christian service, asking ourselves about the extent to which we honor God. What do we mean by that? Is this a matter of respect?; or esteem?; or courteous behavior?; or lofty thoughts? No, the force of this promise is worship. As D. Martyn Lloyd-Jones once observed, "If we want to know God and to be blessed by God, we must start by worshipping Him." This is not a popular preoccupation. For many of us the whole pattern of our lives is upset by the failure to put God where he belongs. So honoring God has much to do with worship and its service outcomes of bowing down, standing up, walking, witnessing and living for him.

Why, then, do we worship? Christians live in a 'what's in it for me?' society. Contrary to the way some might interpret this text, for me it is not about prosperity theology. We do not worship as a route to promotion, preference or position. We are taught in the Bible to honor God because he is God and because we were designed to honor him. Listen to the historic and powerful words of Thomas Aquinas, "We pay God honour and reverence not for His sake (because he is of himself full of glory to which no creature can add anything) but for our sake." We find a similar emphasis in the great words of Augustine:

> *God is neither the better if thou praise Him, nor worse if thou disparage*
> *Him; but thou, by praising Him that is good, art the better: by*
> *disparaging thou art the worse, for He remaineth good as He is.*

Now to a deeper look at how we worship him. Honoring starts with the heart, the center of spiritual life as we have earlier observed. The psalmist helps us to see what this involves, "May the words of my mouth and the meditation of my heart be pleasing in your sight, O LORD, my Rock and my Redeemer."[xxiv] This is a practical, everyday type of honoring. It's in the market place and in the kitchen; in the school and the college; in the train and in the car. But the Bible also cautions against doing this falsely. Did not Jesus say, quoting Isaiah, "These people honor me with their lips, but their hearts are far from me"?[xxv] The struggle for ambition and success can contribute to that passive type of Christian living that knows how to achieve minimum compliance of the lips but little else. Honoring God costs. If practiced, it will show in our personal life of faith, in our promises, in our thanksgiving, in our obedience, and in many other ways. Leon Morris comments on this issue with some considerable edge, "Worship that costs us nothing is worth precisely what it costs."

The word "honor" in Samuel's prophecy literally means "make heavy" and, conversely, "despise" has the sense of "making light." We might view this as an added or subtracted ingredient to our lives. Many ambitious and successful Christian people at times feel that there is something missing, a void, an emptiness in their lives. That sense of having everything, yet having nothing, is part of the spirit of our age. The promise here is to add that ingredient that our world, with all its challenges and stimulation, simply cannot provide. But the promise is conditional, and honoring God requires a right relationship with him, a quietness of spirit and a life based on faith. Our world, with its growing stress on the individual and his or her independence, implicitly challenges all of these elements.

We need to acknowledge, therefore, that there are barriers to honoring God in our lives. So the second part of the verse, "but those who despise me will be disdained," reminds us of our accountability before God and of the eternal dimension of God's planning. This verse is in every sense a benchmark, and we should treat it as such. There are many things around us that we did not set out to worship, but worship them we do. Micah pens a telling verse, "so you will never again worship the work of your own hands."[xxvi] He is, of course, referring to foreign gods of their own design. So, what's new? They are all part of the hindrances to properly honoring God. Without this sort of standard we are unlikely to be able to temper and properly base our ambitions, or determine what God means by success in our lives.

Message 6

1. Review and recalibrate your ambitions in the light of this chapter. What do you find?

2. Look back at the five questions posed in the ambition health check. Write these in a file card, enter them in your computer or Palmpilot, or put them on your office or study wall so that you have to see them at least once a month over the next year. If you do that, you will probably want them there the rest of your life!

3. Consider some of the sacrifices you have already made at the altar of success, whether for good or bad reasons. Repent of any mistakes you have made and ask God to guide you in such decisions in the future.

4. In the light of the promise and the warning in 1 Samuel 2:30, are you truly honoring God in you life? If not, what do you specifically need to change?

Further reading

Bloesch, Donald, *Freedom for Obedience: Evangelical Ethics in Contemporary Times* (San Francisco: Harper & Row, 1987).

Ellsworth, R., *How to Live in a Dangerous World* (Darlington: Evangelical Press, 1998).

Hill, Alexander, *Just Business: Christian Ethics for the Market Place* (Downers Grove, IL: IVP, 1997).

Packer, J. I., *Rediscovering Holiness* (Ann Arbor, MI: Vine Books, 1999).

Endnotes

i   1 Cor. 9:24.

ii   Rom. 12:1.

iii   Phil. 1:21.

iv   Gen. 11:4.

v   Mk. 10:35-45.

vi   Jer. 45:5.

vii   Jas. 3:16.

viii   Gal. 5:20.

ix   Rom. 15:20.

x   Mk. 10:45.

xi   See his book on the beatitudes and the blessed Christian life: Max Lucado, *The Applause of Heaven* (Dallas, TX: Word, 1990).

xii   For a challenging personal perspective on success, read David Short, *Real Success and How to Achieve It* (Fearn, Ross-shire: Christian Focus, 1998).

xiii   Mk. 10:43-44 (TEV).

xiv   Mt. 25:21.

xv   Rev. 5:9.

xvi   1 Cor. 6:20.

xvii   1 Jn. 2:17.

xviii   Lk. 12:13-21

xix   1 Sam. 18:14.

xx   Neh. 2:20.

xxi   1 Chr. 4:10, and see Bruce Wilkinson, *The Prayer of Jabez: Breaking Through to the Blessed Life* (Sisters, OR: Multnomah, 2000).

xxii   Eph. 1:10 (J. B. Phillips, *The New Testament in Modern English* (London: Collins, 1972).

xxiii   1 Sam. 2:30.

xxiv   Ps. 19:14.

xxv   Mk. 7:6.

xxvi   Mic. 5:13 (NLT).

PART THREE
RESPONSIBILITIES

7
Lordship, Grace and the Call of God

"Therefore, I urge you, brothers, in view of God's mercy, to offer your bodies as living sacrifices, holy and pleasing to God – this is your spiritual act of worship." (Rom. 12:1)

Outline   The aim of this chapter, the first of four chapters in Part Three, "Responsibilities," is to help us to acknowledge God's grace, surrender to his lordship, and hear his call at a personal level. It therefore poses some very fundamental questions about how and why we became Christians in the first place. We will ask four different questions.

Is Jesus Christ Lord?
Here we look at the substance of this great Christian creedal statement and affirmation, assessing the impact it should have on our lives.

What is God's call for my life?
In examining the meaning of God's call to all Christians, we look at the specific call to a task through the examples of Isaiah and Nehemiah.

What does the Lord require of me?
The prophet Micah both poses and answers this question. And the answer is a foundational part of preparing to respond to God.

Can I be part of the miracle?
As miracles of grace, we are called to work with the Lord. The attitudes and roles of the disciples in the feeding of the five thousand are explored in a short case study that teaches some powerful lessons.

Is Jesus Christ Lord?   While writing this book, I have been constantly gripped by my total inability to change a single thing in any reader's life – regardless of how or what I write. Yet this book is intended to stimulate a positive change in Christian lifestyles. While I can try to keep it interesting, reflective, direct and challenging, even at times humorous and stimulating, I have no power to change lives. In all of that I am no different from any author. But as a Christian I believe in the power of the word of God to change lives – hence the constant references to the Bible. This chapter goes back to the source of eternal life, back to Christ, back to the call of God in our lives, back to how we first received his mercy. We look at all of this in the knowledge that it takes nothing short of a vision of the Lord to renew our lives. I have long thought that it is Satan's business to keep busy people busy, inducing in them a type of amnesia about the nature and strength of their original commitment to Christ; dulling their sensitivity to the Spirit; blinding them from seeing the face of the Lord; and sapping their mental energies. I have experienced all of these effects, and more.

> *Expect disruption, challenge and conviction – but also expect peace, joy and blessing*

Our first, and very personal, question is whether Jesus Christ is the Lord of our lives. Do we recognize and accept his paramount authority? And how does all of this correspond to our motives and life patterns? There are many "lords" around us everyday, who stake a claim for our worship and service. And there is also a lord within us, who wants to be free to set his own agenda. Charles Colson puts it rather starkly when he states, "If Christ's lordship does not disrupt our own lordship, then the reality of our conversion must be questioned." Yes, Christianity does come with a health warning. Expect disruption, challenge and conviction – but also expect peace, joy and blessing.

"Jesus Christ is Lord" is perhaps the oldest, yet most demanding, of the Christian creeds. The word "lord" was in everyday use referring to a master, owner or employer. As a form of address, "lord" emphasized the power of a superior over an inferior. If you call someone "lord" you are recognizing that person as a leader and implying a willingness to obey him. In many instances, "lord" has simply been used out of politeness. Some people used it of Jesus in that sense. It's just possible that some Christians today use it of him in the same way. It is clear, however, that this was not what the apostles had in mind in verses such as, "For we do not preach ourselves, but Jesus Christ as Lord, and ourselves as your servants for Jesus' sake";[i] "Therefore I tell you that no one who is speaking by the Spirit of God says, 'Jesus be cursed,' and no one can say 'Jesus is Lord,' except by the Holy Spirit";[ii] "But in your hearts set apart Christ as Lord."[iii]

What, then, is the force of this declaration? "Jesus Christ is Lord" incorporates several related ideas on which we need to prayerfully reflect. All of them have something to say to us as we continue to seek an answer to the "whose life is it anyway?" question.

- *Ownership*: We are under new ownership, but still managing ourselves. The title deeds have changed hands, and we have a new Lord. As Paul put it, "You are not your own; you were bought at a price."[iv] A former slave of sin has been bought for freedom and is now the property of the Lord Jesus.

- *Mastery*: In the master/slave relationship, the focus is on control and obedience. This is not a relationship of fear, but one of reverence. Indeed, we respond to the new master with absolute love. There's nothing better than an unsolicited act of profound gratitude.

- *Royalty*: "Lord" was a word of imperial power and, by the end of the first century, it was the normal title for the Roman Emperor. The early Christians used it as a cry of exaltation in their worship, as the community submitted itself to Christ's authority. Among several examples of this is Paul's great discourse on the mind of Christ; "... that at the name of Jesus every knee should bow, in heaven and on earth and under the earth, and every tongue confess that Jesus Christ is Lord, to the glory of God the Father."[v]

- *Deity*: The Jews used it of God, and the pagans used it for cult deities, which is itself a manifestation of the use and abuse to which this title was put. Christians used it to declare the absolute deity of Christ, Son of God and Son of Man. This use is evident in some of the apostles' greetings, where the one Lord Jesus stands in contrast to the many lords of the pagan world.

These different shades of meaning help us to see why this title was both a declaration and an affirmation of what Christians believed and recognized. The title "Lord" brought with it all these connotations and pictures. Such a declaration was not lightly made, and many paid the ultimate price because they would not say that Caesar was lord in times where an emperor's divinity had been proclaimed. To them it was a matter of absolutes in ownership, mastery, royalty and deity. It was, and is, a statement of our worship, our priorities, our values, our core Christian beliefs. In many ways, it is the essence of the essence. It is what separates us from our world. But it has profound consequences. People who say this and mean it are transformed people. As we saw above, none of us can say it in truth, or live it in reality, without the Spirit. Augustine was right and thoroughly biblical when he said, "He values not Christ at all who does not value Christ above all."

How did we come to know this great truth? Only by God's grace. "But when the kindness and love of God our Savior appeared, he saved us, not because of righteous things we had done, but because of his mercy."[vi] Philip Yancey, whose lucid book on grace has been a blessing to so many, observes that grace is the key word of Christianity and the only key to unlocking the meaning of the New Testament.[vii] It's hard to argue with that. My wife, Anna, is a crossword enthusiast. I do not share this hobby, and my contribution is to be in the room when she is working on one, trying to respond to random questions while attempting in vain to do some other reading. On occasion, my domestic credit rating rises when I am able to provide an answer to an improbable or complex clue. The reason? Suddenly all the other clues fall into place, missing letters are provided, and the problem is solved. Grace is like that. When we know about "grace," everything else becomes clearer. God's love reaching us with no strings attached is against all our human instincts. And the great truth is that he came for you and me. Yancey draws attention to that remarkable line in Mozart's *Requiem*, "Remember, merciful Jesu, that I am the cause of your journey." We can be sure that he does remember, but do we? We need a fresh sense of God's love and grace to address the consequences of the lordship of Christ. It cannot be done by *pushing* us into action, but rather by God's Spirit *pulling* us by the magnetic power of Christ.

grace is the key word of Christianity

Why, then, does Jesus have to be Lord? Would something less not suffice? We have to be very clear about this. There are three reasons why Jesus has to be Lord of our lives. The first is simply because of who he is. We do not make him Lord. He is already Lord of everything. The second is because of the relationship he wants to establish with us. The third is because of the work that he wants to accomplish through us. Naming Jesus as Lord is therefore both a cry of submission and an act of confession. It is both a prelude to seeing our whole lives in context, and an ongoing necessity to enable us to keep a focus on what really matters. To put it another way, we are likely to arrive at a very different answer to the question "whose life is it anyway?" when we address it after some major business or professional triumph than if we answer it on our knees before God and with his word in our hands.

> *Naming Jesus as Lord is therefore both a cry of submission and an act of confession*

☑ **ACTION:** It is time to pause and take stock. In a rather sobering exercise of self-examination you might want to prayerfully address the following:

- Which parts of your life do you consider not to be under the lordship of Christ?

- Which parts of your life do you think the Lord wants to take under his lordship?

- For example, is he Lord of your time? Of your talents? Of your material possessions? Of your moral life? Of your future?

- What would have to change to be able to say, "Jesus Christ is now the Lord of my life"?

- If Jesus Christ was really Lord of your life, "whose life would it be anyway?"

What is God's call for my life?

As we become Christians, or as we rededicate ourselves to Christ as Lord, we are confronted by one of the most basic of all biblical truths, namely that God actually *calls* men and women. The Bible expresses this calling in several different ways – for example, we are called by God's grace; called to peace; called into fellowship with Christ; called to freedom.[viii] All of this is wonderful as we reflect on the sovereign Lord taking an interest in people like us. We are all conscious that nothing we have done or can do will make us deserving of being called by God. But as we look further into this concept, and keep in mind the sense of gratitude that we should have, we quickly see that it is also associated with a call to duty. To many, this idea is much less palatable. Many passages in the Bible urge disciples to live their lives in a certain way. Thus, for example: "As a prisoner for the Lord, then, I urge you to live a life worthy of the calling you have received";[ix] "To this you were called, because Christ suffered for you, leaving you an example, that you should follow in his steps."[x] There is no doubt that this concerns our lifestyle, since it is a call to pursue the road of holiness. As John Blanchard says, "Morally, a Christian is called to holiness; dynamically, he is called to service." Romans 12:1, the theme text for this chapter, expresses this superbly. The call of God is intended to meet the response of "a spiritual act of worship." We have all received a summons, as to an office or an honor, an invitation to a privilege, but also a summons to undertake a task. We can summarize the teaching of the Bible by saying that we are called to believe and called to serve. J. I. Packer expresses this perfectly, "Gifts are given to be used, and a capacity to minister in a particular way constitutes a prima facie call to that particular ministry."

Gifts are given to be used

Now we need to stand back and feel the force of this call to a task. The word itself places a powerful obligation on us to answer the voice of God. We often implicitly misinterpret God's call as something that only missionaries, pastors and full-time Christian workers hear. We can easily hide behind that belief and claim (or hope) that the rest of us should not expect to hear from God in this way. If your busy life is anything like mine, you are surrounded by the means of receiving and responding to messages. We develop the necessary skill to quickly distinguish between them, prioritize them, and respond accordingly. So where is God's call and his voice in all this mix of sound? If we were honest, we would admit that it is often drowned in the sea of noise. And many of us have lost our ability, if we ever had it in the first place, to hear God's distinctive and persistent call. It's even worse than that at times, because much of the noise is of our own making. We have to want to hear. As we seek to come to terms with all of this for our own situation, we can learn from some biblical examples of men responding to God's call. Here are two short cases involving very different characters.

☑ **ACTION:** Read Isaiah 6:1-8.

Case 1: Isaiah This is a watershed experience for Isaiah, and these verses read like a checklist for whether or not we have really heard God's call. In Isaiah's case, this vision set the direction for his service. It clearly was not his first experience of God. But this experience reminds me of the profound truth that if we have a right perspective on God, we will have a right perspective on everything else. So what can we learn from these verses?

Isaiah was already worshipping when God spoke to him. The vision came to Isaiah in the temple at a time of national uncertainty, after the long-standing king, Uzziah, had died. Above all, it was a vision of God's holiness. Isaiah's words set out five realities about God that we, too, need to know.

1. *Lordship*: he saw God on a throne.
2. *Greatness*: he saw God high and exalted.
3. *Nearness*: he observed that "the whole earth was full of his glory."
4. *Purity*: he responded with a great sense of his own unworthiness, "Woe to me! I am ruined!"
5. *Mercy*: as the live coal touched his lips, he was assured by God, "See, this has touched your lips; your guilt is taken away and your sin atoned for."

We forget these five things at our peril. Knowing them and remembering them are both critical for hearing and responding to God. To serve God, Isaiah had to be a clean instrument. In his case, he specifically required clean lips, to be deeply aware of the sins of speech – a critical aspect of his calling. This experience took Isaiah into a new relationship with God. It was that, and that alone, which gave new impetus to his service. He responds with that cry, a cry that is music to God's ears, "Here am I. Send me!" He was not coerced. He gave a ready response as a grateful reaction to God's forgiving grace. As J. Hudson Taylor put it, "God uses men who are weak and feeble enough to lean on Him." That was Isaiah's experience; it can also be ours.

☑ **ACTION:** Read Nehemiah 1 – 2:10.

Case 2: Nehemiah   Nehemiah was quite a tough character with lots of energy, but it is interesting to look at his life in terms of vocation and leadership. He combined a personal enthusiasm and a pastoral heart with some practical common sense. What did it take to get Nehemiah to leave his routine but honored palace job with king Artaxerxes and take on all the risks entailed in becoming Jerusalem's governor, builder and spiritual leader? We might view this as a high-risk career move, with lots of potential downside. But Nehemiah answered the call of God, as reflected in a number of aspects of his life.

- *Consecration to God*: He identified himself as God's servant. As such, he was sensitive to God's approach to him and ready to receive his guidance. For Nehemiah and for all of us, this is the crucial first step in responding to God's call.

- *Communication of the needs of his people*: Nehemiah had a burden to respond to a real need in Jerusalem. His emotions were touched, and his heart moved.

- *God's interests were his interests*: When he heard of the situation, "I sat down and wept. For some days I mourned and fasted ..."[xi] God was not being glorified and praised in his great city. Something needed to be done.

- *Continuous prayer*: For at least three months after he heard the call, he and his friends were in prayer. They asked each day that God would act, but he kept them praying. Finally, Nehemiah was released to go to Jerusalem in an amazing and unprecedented way. After all, he was a slave.

Nehemiah is later shown to have that distinctive combination of knowing both the role of prayer and the role of the sword, as he faced many enemies who would have derailed his mission. Lots of us might well share with him that practical "get up and go" personality that God utilized to such good effect in this man. But do we share his holiness and his dedication to the task to which God called him? Do we bring to such tasks all the energies, time and enthusiasm that have been so central to our secular prosperity? Invariably not. So, in that sense, we regularly rob God of what is his.

☑ **ACTION:** Stop to consider what these two cases have to teach you about God's call to individuals. Compare and contrast the situation in which you currently find yourself with those of Isaiah and Nehemiah. Try to recall the times when you have logged a call from God, hearing him through Bible reading or preaching, but have not made a positive response.

What does the Lord require of me?

In order to respond to this question regarding God's requirements, we will examine a question that Micah both posed and answered. This passage greatly helps us in getting an answer to our core question, "whose life is it anyway?" We often pose rhetorical questions, even to God, but do not expect answers. One of the most casual throwaway social questions is, "How are you?" This question looks for little response besides general pleasantries. I have a friend who often responds to that question by asking either "Do you really want to know?" or "How much time do you have to listen?" Similarly, we have to be serious in our quest for an answer. Because, if we are really serious, God could change our lives.

So we consider Micah's words. "And what does the LORD require of you? To act justly and to love mercy and to walk humbly with your God."[xii] This great text captures the essence of the life of true devotion. The Lord had made it clear that he did not want external rituals from Israel, but he did want the offering of sanctified lives. He still wants worshippers who express that in relationships rather than in "religion" for its own sake. Micah makes his point in the language of the courtroom. Israel is being charged, God is the judge, and Micah his counsel. Israel, in effect, asks (as we often do in our better moments), "what can we do to put things right with God?" They had assumed that the solution lay in ritual offerings, but that was not what God wanted – hence our text.

There may well be some parallels between our own situation and this passage. We might be very willing to offer God something he does not seek and to which he attributes no value. This "offering" may well have value to us. We might, for example, offer time or money, but in the wrong spirit. We might offer a grand, public gesture of support such as sponsoring a major event for a Christian cause, when what he wants is much less visible but more durable. We might offer ritual church attendance, without committing our hearts to his service. More fundamentally, perhaps, we may not like this question simply because it assumes that God places requirements on his people. If you are of that view, try not to deflect the force of this message – because God does clearly have many expectations of us as followers of Christ. So what did the Lord want here?

We might be very willing to offer God something he does not seek

- *To act justly*: This is one of the major virtues of God, so it is not surprising that the Lord requires it of his disciples. This virtue involves a series of commitments to the community in which we live and work. Among other things it asks us to assume a sense of responsibility for weaker members of society; it insists on the rights of others; it requires honesty and uprightness with people; and so much more. You will note that what is required is for the people to act – not to theorize about justice. There was ample evidence in Israel that there was a problem with this. Thus the striking words of Amos, "But let justice roll on like a river, righteousness like a never-failing stream!"[xiii] This injunction has much to say to us in terms of our approach to evaluating people, criticizing others, responding to need, implementing commercial practices, and maintaining integrity in relationships of all kinds. D. L. Moody said, "Of 100 men, one will read the Bible, the 99 will read the Christian."

- *Love mercy*: At its root, mercy is kindness. It goes beyond justice to areas of life where no giving is required. In that sense, it is close to grace. Perhaps it is best expressed as a word of partnership, reflecting both God's faithfulness to us and our faithfulness to God. Here is one of the Christian faith's transmitted qualities – as we have received, so we behave to others with mercy. The psalmist reminds us, "For great is his love toward us, and the faithfulness of the LORD endures forever."[xiv] The verb in this text is very important – we have to *love* mercy. In this phrase there is once again a communal obligation. Thomas Adam put that as follows, "He that demands mercy and shows none ruins the bridge over which he has to pass himself."

- *Walk humbly with your God*: This style of daily walk goes hand in hand with the practice of justice and mercy. It implies living in humble fellowship with God. These three aspects of character are part of the foundations of a Christian lifestyle. This issue of a careful walk with God is central to us, since it is a recurring theme throughout the Bible. For example, as we have seen, Paul urges the Ephesians, "Be very careful, then, how you live – not as unwise but as wise, making the most of every opportunity, because the days are evil."[xv]

Now we need to stand back and review our behavior in the light of these requirements. It is worth noting that the first two items are readily found in many people who are not Christians. But the third is unique to Christians, and the combination of the three can only be achieved by the power of the Spirit in our lives. Clearly this text does not contain the whole canon of the Bible on discipleship, but it is a powerful reminder of the need to get the fundamentals right. These qualities are part of the foundation we need in order to respond to God's call and upon which we need to base our service for him. Without such building blocks, it is hard to see evidence of new creation in us. A part of the "whose life is it anyway?" question concerns the extent to which the surrendered life is becoming more Christ-like.

☑ **ACTION:** Suppose that Micah 6:8 was to be used to diagnose the presence or absence of Christianity in your life, as assessed by your peers.

What would be the likely outcome?

You might call "foul" on this question, claiming that your peers are not your judges. This is true, but they are assessing and evaluating us every day if we actively profess faith in Christ. They may have already arrived at their own answer as to whose life ours actually is by observing our behavior.

Rather sobering, isn't it?

Can I be part of the miracle? We end this chapter with a great story for busy Christian people. It is amazing that God can take people like us and use us for his glory. We begin by acknowledging that every Christian is a miracle of God's grace. We continue by accepting that God wants us to be part of his ongoing miraculous work. As Ron Dunn said, a miracle can be defined as "God doing what only God can do." To illustrate this point, let's look at Jesus feeding the five thousand.

☑ **ACTION:** Read Mark 6:30-44

The context is important for us. The disciples have returned, exhausted, from a period of mission. They are looking forward to a time of reporting, relaxing and replenishing their energies. The Lord invites them to do just that. It was clear that there was so much pressure and noise around them that they had time for neither leisure nor food. So it's vacation time at last. If you are like me, all this sounds rather familiar. The one thing we try hard not to interrupt is our hard-earned holiday. They were just the same. So they set sail with Jesus, heading towards the east side of the Sea of Galilee to a place where they could get some rest. Imagine their reaction when they come in sight of the shore, and there is a vast welcoming party anxious to meet Jesus. "That was a short vacation!" Or, more likely, "Oh no! I thought we were here to relax with Jesus." The Bible doesn't tell us what they think at this stage, but subsequent events only too clearly reveal their feelings. They were definitely groaning inside.

Jesus' reaction contrasts sharply to this. In no sense is he disgruntled. He sees into the hearts of the large crowd. His twofold reaction is classic, revealing the very center of the gospel. First, he shows love and compassion to them; secondly, he brings his unique perspective to them, describing them as sheep without a shepherd. In short, the disciples and their Lord are on a different wavelength. How often is that true of us as well?

Jesus' compassion extends to wanting to feed the crowd. Now we know for sure how the disciples *really* feel. They burst out with some aggression ... it's remote, it's late, there's a lot of them, there's no food and it would cost a fortune to get some anyway ... so send them all home. In the middle of this assessment of the situation, Jesus stuns them further by telling them to feed the crowd. We might think that their reaction was reasonable, but we would have to acknowledge that they calculated without Christ. What they said made sense, but it was not good spiritual arithmetic. Quite often today the Lord asks us to take food of one kind or another to people, and we react in a similar way. We who call Christ Lord always need to be ready to respond to his call, whether or not it suits our schedule.

We who call Christ Lord always need to be ready to respond to his call

The Lord then takes the basic resource that is available, blesses it and offers the crowd food. All of us are just small beginnings in his hands. In effect, Jesus instructs the crowd to sit before him and be blessed. But there is something else that is remarkable here. The disciples, in spite of their attitude, indifference and incredulity, are invited to take the fish and the loaves to the people. It was by their hands that the miracle became evident to the crowd. It wasn't their miracle, but the Lord was gracious enough to invite them to be part of it. Now is that not truly remarkable? What an encouragement that is for us. Not always the best of disciples; sometimes finding it hard to catch the vision; more than a little lacking in faith; often tired and under pressure, we too can work with him by his invitation. In this incident, the miraculous supply of God's grace was limited only by the number of consumers. As beneficiaries of that same grace, we in turn are asked to serve with him and for him.

Message 7

1. Set aside time to carefully consider how this chapter has caused you to think (or rethink) the push and pull aspects of God's personal call to you.

2. Reflect on the theme text in Romans 12:1. How would you describe your present "spiritual act of worship"?

3. Reflect on the profound consequences of declaring that "Jesus Christ is Lord." Ask the Lord to embed the meaning of this declaration of faith in your heart and in your life.

4. Look out for a miracle nearby that God would like you to be a part of.

Further reading

Barclay, William, *Crucified and Crowned* (London: SCM, 1961).

Cole, Michael, *He is Lord* (London: Hodder & Stoughton, 1987).

Packer, J. I., *Knowing God* (London: Hodder & Stoughton, 1973).

Yancey, Philip, *Reaching for the Invisible God: What Can We Expect to Find?* (Grand Rapids, MI: Zondervan, 2000).

Endnotes

  i 2 Cor. 4:5.

  ii 1 Cor. 12:3.

  iii 1 Pet. 3:15.

  iv 1 Cor. 6:19-20.

  v Phil. 2:10-11.

  vi Tit. 3:4-5.

  vii Philip Yancey, *What's So Amazing about Grace?* (Grand Rapids, MI: Zondervan, 1997).

  viii See Gal. 1:6, Col. 3:15, 1 Cor. 1:9, Gal. 5:13.

  ix Eph. 4:1.

  x 1 Pet. 2:21.

  xi Neh. 1:4.

  xii Mic. 6:8.

  xiii Amos 5:24.

  xiv Ps. 117:2.

  xv Eph. 5:15-16.

8
Time Out for Review and Response

"For I am the LORD, your God, who takes hold of your right hand and says to you, Do not fear; I will help you." (Isa. 41:13)

Outline One of our responsibilities as disciples is to take time out for review and response. Such reflection requires a reasonable amount of time, but in the midst of our busy lives we rarely set that time aside. Assuming that time has been allocated for this purpose, this chapter offers guidance on how we might consider the appropriate response to three different questions.

How have I responded?
Based on the formal secular reviews in which we take part, we examine our own response to God; learn lessons from others; and check with the Lord to see what he asks us to respond to.

How could I respond better?
The biblical examples of Simon Peter, who was called at a time of failure, and the Hebrew Christians, as they responded to Christ's sacrifice, teach us more about our response to God.

What do I do if I really fail?
By looking at the classic, yet extreme, case of David, we learn from Psalm 51 about his way back to fellowship with and service for God.

How have I responded?   Throughout the various action points and messages in this book, we have consistently been challenged to respond to God's call upon our lives. At different points in our lives many of us will also have experienced teaching sessions, Bible studies, discussions groups, special missions, church weekends, conventions, pastoral appeals, and so on, which have challenged our faith and response. It's just possible that reading this book has brought echoes of such occasions to mind, and hopefully you are now ready for the difficult task of serious personal assessment. Each person will come to this exercise with a different perspective. "Nothing new here, quite interesting, but I am in reasonably good shape," you might say, or "My lifestyle is too crowded to give anything else to the Lord; I am a disciple, but a rather distant one"; or "This exercise really does challenge me, but I've been here before, and I have not been able to sustain a reshaping of my life pattern"; or even, "My life is a mess. It's not at all obvious on the outside, but my answer to your question is, I'm not certain who owns my life. It's not me, but it's not God either. He really is at the edge." These are all common reactions to this topic. Mike Yaconelli brought his own experience (and honesty) to the task that confronts us when he said,

> My life is a mess. After forty-five years of trying to follow Jesus, I keep losing him in the crowded busyness of my life ... I have had temporary successes and isolated moments of closeness to God, but I long for the continuing presence of Jesus moment by moment. Yet most of the moments of my life seem hopelessly stuck in a tangled web of obligations and distractions.[i]

I suspect that these feelings ring true with many of us.

In our busy lives there is rarely time for review. There is, however, usually sufficient time for frustration and a sense of guilt over what might have been. We probably direct more attention to our annual employment appraisal than to any spiritual appraisal. Assessment interviews occur at regular intervals in the secular world – forms are completed, formal feedback is given, targets are set, development opportunities are identified. This is all part of the stock in trade of getting the best out of people, supporting them in their employment and ensuring their employability. Our point of departure here, then, is one that we will all recognize. When was the last time we went through a process of self-appraisal and review of our Christian lives? Some of us may discuss these issues formally (or informally) with others whom we trust. The presumption here is neither of success nor of failure. All of us have a mixed experience of loyalty to the Lord. The bigger question is whether the future could be more worthy of his commendation than some parts of our past.

> ☑ **ACTION:** The central "whose life is it anyway?" question remains before us. Have you answered that question differently at different stages of your Christian life? And have these answers been evident in the way you have actually lived your life? After all Christianity is a set of beliefs that are intended to behave!

Assessment invariably involves measuring a response to a set of objectives, tasks or targets over a period of time. We may or may not see our self-assessment of our Christian progress in that way. Indeed, we may reject the very thought that the Lord has set objectives before us and have therefore not registered or acknowledged them in the past. If this is so, then we need to go back to basics. A frequent criticism of individuals in secular performance reviews is that they lack ambition or hunger – basically, they do not succeed because they do not want to. This is also true in Christian life. We often identify it as a lack of commitment. Jesus highlights this in his remarkable words in the beatitudes, "Blessed are those who hunger and thirst for righteousness, for they will be filled."[ii] This is a powerful metaphor, especially when you consider that extremes of hunger and thirst constantly threatened the lives of many people in the ancient world, as they sadly do in many parts of our world today. There is great intensity in what Jesus says here, and it has much to say about the Christian life. This is not about missing a meal or a morning coffee break, or even about a period of fasting. This is a hunger and thirst of the soul. Desiring righteousness really is a matter of

Desiring righteousness really is a matter of life and death

life and death. It is demanding, and busy people often do not feel the weight of that demand because it is only one demand among many. Yet there is also great encouragement here for us all. The hungering and thirsting, namely the attitude of the heart, is in itself blessed. Jesus is not saying that we have to attain this righteousness in order to receive the blessing. As Thomas à Kempis says, "Man sees the deed, but God sees the intention." But we have to want to hear and respond. Our heart has to be in this. God calls us to have a right relationship with him, and he promises happiness and the prospect of being filled. There is further mystery and wonder in this blessing, however, in that the Lord wants that intensity of desire to stay with us. John Blanchard develops that thought when he says, "God promises to fill those who hunger and thirst after righteousness, yet the sign that he is doing so is that they go on hungering and thirsting." Let's pray that may be true of all of us. Without this desire in our hearts, a product of the Spirit, we will never respond to God as he wants us to.

We need the Spirit to stimulate our spiritual appetites

As we review how we have responded, and check our hunger for God's ways, we must remember the vital work of the Spirit in preparing our minds and hearts. This links us back to the question of stewardship discussed in Chapter 3. There we were reminded that all we have is really his, but we don't always remember that. We need the Spirit to stimulate our spiritual appetites. In order to properly function, we need the following degree of empowerment and more.

Open eyes: "The man without the Spirit does not accept the things that come from the Spirit of God, for they are foolishness to him, and he cannot understand them, because they are spiritually discerned."[iii] All Christians, but especially busy ones, can be tainted by the influence of non-Christians and behave like the person without the Spirit. Closed eyes miss service opportunities.

Quickened faculties: "The Spirit gives life; the flesh counts for nothing. The words I have spoken to you are spirit and they are life."[iv] Jesus spoke these words when he was faced with many disciples deserting him. His teaching was tough and demanding, and some were just not up for it. Only if we are open to the influence of the Spirit can we perceive divine things.

Sensitive ears: "The Sovereign LORD has opened my ears, and I have not been rebellious; I have not drawn back."[v] We spend so much time listening to everything else, we need to pray that the Lord will help us distinguish his voice from the noise around us.

Alert minds: "We demolish arguments and every pretension that sets itself up against the knowledge of God, and we take captive every thought to make it obedient to Christ."[vi] Paul had a powerful intellect and was a unique apologist for the cause of Christ. Few of us may be like him, but more than ever today Christ's followers need to be both engaged in society and willing to commit their minds to his affairs.

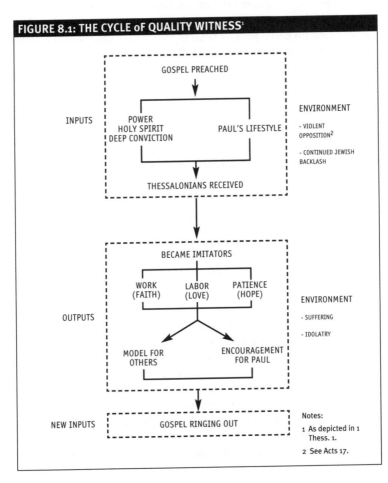

FIGURE 8.1: THE CYCLE of QUALITY WITNESS[1]

INPUTS

GOSPEL PREACHED

POWER
HOLY SPIRIT
DEEP CONVICTION

PAUL'S LIFESTYLE

THESSALONIANS RECEIVED

ENVIRONMENT

- VIOLENT OPPOSITION[2]

- CONTINUED JEWISH BACKLASH

BECAME IMITATORS

WORK (FAITH)   LABOR (LOVE)   PATIENCE (HOPE)

OUTPUTS

MODEL FOR OTHERS

ENCOURAGEMENT FOR PAUL

ENVIRONMENT

- SUFFERING

- IDOLATRY

NEW INPUTS

GOSPEL RINGING OUT

Notes:

1 As depicted in 1 Thess. 1.

2 See Acts 17.

The New Testament gives us some excellent examples of what this all looks like in practice. Paul commended the church at Thessalonica for living this out, "We continually remember before our God and Father your work produced by faith, your labor prompted by love, and your endurance inspired by hope in our Lord Jesus Christ."[vii] Their spiritual awareness and hunger had led them to display both virtues and activities that brought honor to God. By God's grace, we can all do the same.

The Thessalonian church is such a good example for us, that the detail of their witness is summarized in Figure 8.1. I have called it "a cycle of quality witness" with inputs, outputs and resulting new inputs as they lived for God. As the figure suggests, the environment was not favorable and the social pressures very real. But they became imitators and good role models. There was no doubt about the quality of their response or about how effective it was. They lived as if they knew the correct answer to our central question.

☑ **ACTION:** Test yourself against the four characteristics above. How does such an exercise heighten your sense of dependence on the work of the Spirit? The hymn by Edwin Hatch serves as a timely prayer for us all.

"Breathe on me, breath of God;
Fill me with life anew,
That I may love what thou dost love,
And do what thou wouldst do."

In all of this discussion about our response to God, we might ask what it is, exactly, that God has designed us to respond to. We do not have far to look. The Christian life is first and foremost a response to the one who died for us in love. If our response is feeble, then we need to look first at our love. As we have seen, we can try to explain away our poor performance by citing endless other variables. All of them miss the essential truth. If we love Christ, our devotion will not remain a secret. This love will show in the spirit and purpose of our lives. One of the finest statements of this is from Matthew Henry, "Love is the root, obedience is the fruit." Given that our responsive love is intended to be *the* key driver of our behavior, how are we to gauge our response to God? There are at least three elements to consider in our personal "compare and contrast" exercise.

The Christ: There is simply no servant and no service like this. By this standard, we all fail. The miracle is that he wants us to work in fellowship with him, and so he set out an amazing brief for all his followers. "Therefore go and make disciples of all nations, baptizing them in the name of the Father and of the Son and of the Holy Spirit, and teaching them to obey everything I have commanded you. And surely I am with you always, to the very end of the age."[viii] This is a directive for all ages, all eras, all cultures from the Sovereign Lord himself. Christians ignore it at their peril.

The cross: Here we confront the ultimate act of sacrifice, against which anything we are called to do pales into insignificance. As John Stott observes, "What dominated his mind was not the living but the giving of His life. This final self-sacrifice was His 'hour' for which He had come into the world."[ix] We often talk about focus and dedication to tasks in our secular lives, and often with some pride. Next time you are tempted to do so, think of the cross. Stott is right to say that we will never see the cross as something done for us until we see it as something done by us.

The call: In Chapter 7 we saw the strength and intention of God's call. The words of Edward Everett Hale reinforce this:

I am only one, but I am one.
I cannot do everything, but
I can do something.
And what I can do, I ought to do.
And what I ought to do, by the
Grace of God, I shall do.

There is little doubt that if we were prepared to respond in faith to the inherent, but awesome, challenges of the Christ, the cross, and the call, we would immediately know the answer to "whose life is it anyway?" Finding the answer by this route, and holding firmly to it, would undoubtedly be life changing.

**How could I
respond better?** The matters we have just been considering may
leave us with a total sense of inadequacy. We might
even conclude that failure is certain and poor
performance the norm, so no effort on our part would be worthwhile. All that
would be true if we were asked to do anything for God in our own strength,
but this is not the case. Equally, if we were motivated by fear, rather than by
love, we would miss the whole point of Christian service. Dominic Smart
makes some thought-provoking points on this, as he cautions against
putting what we do before what we are.[x] He notes that when our
discipleship is task-oriented rather than relationship-oriented, fear and
insecurity motivate our service. The result is a hectic mix of Christian,
secular and family activity in which being Christian disappears under a
burden of activity. This state of affairs is clearly to be avoided, but it is quite
widespread. So let us emphasize that the central issue is how we relate to
Christ our Lord. We are to expect a call to service and respond in love,
knowing that he is entirely capable of guiding us to a work/life balance of
his design – if we will only allow him so to do.

The following two biblical illustrations will further clarify these ideas and
also help to encourage you as you arrive at your own response.

☑ **ACTION::** Read Luke 5:1-11

Case 1: Simon Peter Jesus meets Simon at a point of failure. His
boat is empty of fish, even after a long hard
night of fishing. He has been very busy. He is doubtless impatient, tired
and frustrated. Then a passing teacher instructs him to go back into deep
water. What was his state of mind when that reached his ears? We don't
actually know, but he is polite and in his weakness he obeys. Simon has run
out of ideas for that day's market. In effect, the Lord invades his life and
turns his way of thinking upside-down. When the bountiful fish harvest is
collected, Peter falls at the Lord's feet. He calls him Lord, and in his
presence he immediately realizes his sinful nature. Simon sees that it is the
Lord who has done the catching – he only threw the net. Jesus then invites
him to catch men and become a partner in the Lord's business. How do we
measure Simon's performance? He did all that was necessary by starting

empty-handed; by being wholly obedient; by acknowledging that Jesus was Lord; by confessing his sinful nature; and by being willing to follow him. We can do no more or no less! As the New Testament shows, Simon had his bad times thereafter, failing to meet the Lord's expectations of him on several occasions, but he persevered to be a stalwart of the Christian church.

☑ **ACTION:** Read Hebrews 10:19-39

Case 2: Hebrew Christians   This passage, which comes after much teaching and instruction to the Hebrew Christians, is about their response to all they have heard. It's a call to persevere in Christian life in the light of Christ's sacrifice. In the context, it was a specific call to them to separate from ritual and forms of temple service without regret, because there was something far better – new life in Christ. Many of the themes in this book have been about separation and rebalancing our lives towards God's ends more than we might have done in the past. The critical point of departure for these people was to enter into God's presence in prayer. This is the necessary starting point for us, too. They were told to enter with confidence, feeling completely at home in God's presence; with gratitude, remembering the cost of entering that was paid by Christ the Lord; and with sincerity, in a manner that was wholehearted and not in any way mechanical. These are set out as a precondition to making a response to God. And so this is a call for us to devote some serious time to prayer in order to determine how we should react. These verses in Hebrews outline five elements of our response to God. Every one of them has something to say to the "whose life?" question.

enter with confidence, feeling completely at home in God's presence

Response of closeness: "Let us draw near to God with a sincere heart in full assurance of faith …" (v. 22). The condition of a sincere heart refers to the whole of the inner life of a person. God has to own every part of us; and it is only by trusting God that we can ever draw near to him at all. Busyness may have distanced us, and it may also have led to a loss of stillness in our inner life. In extreme cases, busyness leads us to completely lose our God-consciousness. We need that back if we are ever to be close to God again. James Cabot once observed, "We cannot get away from God, though we can ignore him." Not likely for Christians, you may think – but I wonder.

Response of tenacity: "Let us hold unswervingly to the hope we profess, for he who promised is faithful" (v. 23). This hope was to be an "anchor for the soul," as the writer to the Hebrews says later in the book. Our world is full of false anchors used by stricken human vessels. And most of us rub shoulders each working day with people who are clinging on to them. We have to make sure we do not drift alongside them and lose our real hope. Christians are to be tenacious in hope, remembering that it is the Lord who took the initiative to find us in the first place.

Response of practical Christianity: "Let us consider how we may spur one another on towards love and good deeds" (v. 24). What is the effect of our knowing other Christians? And of them knowing us? This is a great picture of mutual activity and it comes as a Christian obligation, part of our role in the community of Christ. Being too busy and preoccupied in other directions can mean that even this basic contribution is lost – to the detriment of both others and ourselves. We can even watch this going on in our Christian community as a spectator, when the Lord makes it clear he wants a participator. John Wesley's injunction is unforgettable: "Do all the good you can; in all the ways you can; to all the people you can; as long as you can."

Response of fellowship: "Let us not give up meeting together, as some are in the habit of doing ..." (v. 25). Perhaps some of the people the writer refers to here stayed away because they did not regard Christianity as God's complete and final revelation. Today it is often excessive busyness, rather than theology, that can be a powerful enemy to Christian fellowship. Christians are not designed to fly in solo formation. Fellowship is essential, and it is part of our response to the Lord. J. I. Packer expresses this principle with great clarity, "We were neither made nor redeemed for self-sufficient aloneness."

> *Today it is often excessive busyness, rather than theology, that can be a powerful enemy to Christian fellowship*

Response of encouragement: "... but let us encourage one another – and all the more as you see the Day approaching"(v. 25). The ministry of encouragement is wonderful – so open and beneficial to all. It can take many forms – taking a close interest in a person's well-being, giving thanks, showing gratitude, working together in service, giving advice, and so on. Perhaps more people fail from lack of encouragement than from anything else – even in Christian communities. The church and its members should be communities of encouragement, with each of us playing our respective roles in this ministry. As someone once wisely said, "If you wish to be disappointed, look at others; if you wish to be disheartened, look at yourself; if you wish to be encouraged, look to Jesus." As his servants, may we all pray that our Christ-likeness is such that we point others to him by our lives and witness.

☑ **ACTION:** Take the five responses from the call to the Hebrew Christians and use them as a "health check." How would you score by these measures?

What do I do if I really fail?

At this stage in the chapter your need may not have been covered or your case mentioned. In short, you may regard yourself as a complete failure in the "whose life is it anyway?" stakes. Your response may have been well short of your own standards, let alone those of the Lord. You may be justified in your assessment because the Spirit has convicted you through what you have been reading. Yet it is not my intention to take any reader on a track to spiritual depression. There are many excellent biblical examples of failures that turned to great success, one of which (Simon Peter) we have already mentioned. Oswald Chambers stated this well when he said, "Beware of succumbing to failure as inevitable; make it the stepping stone to success." Perhaps the classic biblical case of failure is David, and his experience has much to teach us about actually facing up to our failures. God pressed for a response from David, but it took some time to come. Although you may feel that David's case is a bit extreme, and in no way to be compared to any sense of failure that you may have, I suggest that you be patient and read on.

☑ **ACTION:** Read Psalm 51

This Psalm finds David in the depths of guilt about his moral failure. Murder, adultery and deception are among his crimes. But this dark moment of self-knowledge is also the time when the light of confession, salvation and hope shines through. And what caused this transformation? As always, it was the word of the Lord – in this case through Nathan. When no one else would, or could, Nathan spoke directly to David's heart. We need the same – someone to speak honestly to us. And we also need to hear their words as from God. Such messages may come by various routes, but the Lord's intention is always the same – to bring us to a point where we will hear and obey. Derek Kidner, that superb commentator on the Psalms, says of Psalm 51 that it "has shown generations of sinners the way home, long after they had thought themselves beyond recall." Now that's what I call encouragement!

Let's look at what David had to do to find his way back.

Appeal (vv. 1-2): He calls to God for mercy in the light of his love. His language is that of someone who has no claim to receive any of the favor he seeks. He would like, if possible, for his sins to be struck off the record, and he calls for washing and cleansing of his whole person. Notice that David starts with a deep consciousness of the guilt that makes him unfit to be in God's presence at all. Like it or not, this is where we all have to start. Our guilt may be nothing like his, our sins nothing so heinous. But not responding to the Lord's call is also a serious matter in his eyes. And our attitude to where we are is crucial.

Confession (vv. 3-5): God knew about David's sin long before he confessed it. But now David actually acknowledges it – perhaps for the first time. His crime was adultery against Bathsheba and the murder of Uriah, but ultimately it was sin against God. His conscience is now alerted to this. Forgiveness from God is always free, but confession is rarely easy. It wasn't for David. But confession is necessary for renewed fellowship with God. David was once interested only in hiding his crime; now he is bemused as to how he could ever have treated God like that. It is equally likely that we will need to confess our sins to God before we can sort out the "whose life?" issue.

Restoration (vv. 6-9): There was a huge gap between what David had confessed to doing and how God wanted him to behave. "Surely you desire truth in the inner parts."[xi] But the beginnings of a new future are here, the way to pardon and joy. David wants to be clean, to be taught, and to be washed whiter than snow. The tone is one of the outcast returning, and welcome and festivity are both in the air. God's grace has always been amazing. As Thomas à Kempis says, "When you feel that all is lost, sometimes the greatest gain is ready to be yours."

God's grace has always been amazing

Inner renewal (vv. 10-13): Now to the heart of the matter, "Create in me a pure heart, O God, and renew a steadfast spirit within me."[xii] C. H. Spurgeon grasped the sense of this when he interpreted David's cry as "get the Creator back in me again" – almost as if David was a shell into which God had to come again with new freshness. Sound familiar? Many of us need to go back to first principles, but we are often reluctant so to do. David pleads with God not to regard him as worthless; to grant him a willing spirit; and to sustain him. He knows that his prosperity and affluence have sapped his will to obey God. He wants the joy of God's salvation restored. But there is something even more incredible in these verses. He commits himself to testimony to others, "Then I will teach transgressors your ways, and sinners will turn back to you";[xiii] thus giving us an insight into the positive role of the pardoned sinner with all his experiences and scars. Of course, this is precisely where we all come in. It is incredible to think of the harvest for God still being reaped from this Psalm even today – and of the role that we in turn might play for the remainder of our lives.

Worship and prayer (vv. 14-19): David's conscience had silenced him. He was alive and prospering, but not functioning for God. And so he asks the Lord to open his lips again. David would have sacrificed the cattle from a thousand fields if this would have met God's need, but that was not what God required. His obstinate pride has gone, now he is a penitent worshipper. Our peers may despise a weeping penitent, but God does not. David knew what God was looking for. "The sacrifices of God are a broken spirit; a broken and contrite heart, O God, you will not despise."[xiv] The Psalm ends with the prayer of the people. The effect of a renewed leader's influence is evident in the behavior of his people. Above all, he has an overwhelming sense of gratitude that proceeds to reshape his life.

Here, then, are the lessons from David's encounter with God. The abounding mercy of God is met by the contrition of David. In some ways the process of facing our failures is an ongoing matter for all of us. But the pressures on all of our lives, and our tendency to self-sufficiency, both contribute to us avoiding the crunch review with God that was the key to David's recovery. And someone brought him the message from the Lord. Perhaps we, too, should look out for the bearers of the message of response, and not shun the messenger.

☑ **ACTION:** Consider the particular challenges that this study of review and response has brought to you. You might like to write down the various messages that God has been sending to you on this subject over the past few years. They may have come from the Bible or from other Christians. When you do that, measure your reactions to them.

Message 8

1. Set aside time for a thorough and prayerful review of your Christian discipleship to date.

2. If the joy of Christ is missing from your life, ask the Lord what it would take to bring it back. David's cry in Psalm 51:12 was, "Restore to me the joy of your salvation and grant me a willing spirit, to sustain me."

3. Consider the specific ways that the Christ, the cross and the call have actually impacted your lifestyle this week. Write them down and pray over them.

4. Given all you know about David's life, if he came to teach in your church about recovery and spiritual renewal, would you listen to him? God did, and forgave him. Remember that there is always a way back.

5. Reread our theme text for this chapter, Isaiah 41:13, and think about the help you personally need from God right now.

Further reading

Cymbala, Jim, *Fresh Faith* (Grand Rapids, MI: Zondervan, 1999).

Nouwen, Henri J. M., *The Return of the Prodigal Son: A Story of Homecoming* (London: Darton, Longman & Todd, 1994).

Kendall, R. T., *Total Forgiveness: Achieving God's Greatest Challenge* (London: Hodder & Stoughton, 2001).

Swindoll, Charles R., *Improving Your Serve* (London: Hodder & Stoughton, 1981).

Endnotes

i Mike Yaconelli, *Messy Spirituality: Christianity for the Rest of Us* (London: Hodder & Stoughton, 2000).

ii Mt. 5:6.

iii 1 Cor. 2:14.

iv Jn. 6:63.

v Isa. 50:5.

vi 2 Cor. 10:5.

vii 1 Thess. 1:3.

viii Mt. 28:19-20.

ix John Stott, *The Cross of Christ* (Leicester: IVP, 1986).

x Dominic Smart, *When We Get it Wrong* (Carlisle: Paternoster, 2001).

xi Ps. 51:6.

xii Ps. 51:10.

xiii Ps. 51:13.

xiv Ps. 51:17.

9
Making Choices:
Past, Present and Future

"But if serving the LORD seems undesirable to you, then choose for yourselves this day whom you will serve, whether the gods your forefathers served beyond the River, or the gods of the Amorites, in whose land you are living. But as for me and my household, we will serve the LORD."
(Josh. 24:15)

Outline   We all have to make choices every day, but how many of us realize that decision-making is also one of our Christian responsibilities? In earlier chapters we have alluded to the decisions we make concerning our lifestyles; we now turn to the practical matters associated with making these choices. Here we consider the nature and implications of our past choices; explore the activity of the Christian mind that makes them; and search for some strategic principles to inform our future choices.

What choices have I made?
The focus here is on past choices that have impacted our Christian witness and service. Several practical cases stimulate us to think through our own situations. We consider career and other choices, as well as the nature of both pre- and post-salvation decisions.

What's on my mind?
The activities and preoccupations of our minds influence our behavior – thus thinking and living are connected in a special way for Christians. It is a challenge for all of us to have the mind of Christ and to give him lordship over our minds.[i]

> **Which principles should guide my future choices?**
> This final section aims to refocus our sight on the future by exploring three basic principles to guide us: tithing; jubilee; and fellowship. Applied together, these could bring radical change to many of our lives.

What choices have I made? As we have seen, asking the "whose life is it anyway?" question brings into focus the fact that we have all made choices about how to live our lives – and that we still have other such choices to make. To some degree, we are all products of past choices. Some of these choices were made for us; many were made by us. We probably were not even conscious of making some of these choices, or of their future implications. We may wish that we had been able to make choices at different points, but events conspired against us. Christians know that the paramount life choice is to accept Christ as Savior and Lord. But many choices before and since that one have also shaped our lives. Although we know that we should regard the choice of the Lord as primary and all others as secondary, which of us would be bold enough to say that we always thought that way, or that we did not feel the pressures from some of these lesser choices on a daily basis? As Barnard Meltzer says, "God asks no one whether he will accept life. This is not the choice. The only choice you have as you go through life is how you will live it." We could debate long and hard about where the weight of choice has been in our own individual circumstances. That could lead us down a route of regret and recrimination; or along the path of pride and self-congratulation. But that would be fruitless. There are, however, some specific aspects of this topic that we need to further explore. To prompt us to think through the consequences of past choices, we will look at five different cases based on quotations from Christians I have met. The examples that I have chosen are mainly to do with careers and jobs. I offer comments, but no judgments, on these cases. We are all in the learning business.

we know that we should regard the choice of the Lord as primary and all others as secondary

Case 1: "God put me in this job; it's impossibly busy, and I try to serve him wholeheartedly in this role. The choice was his. I really feel that this is my ministry." Many busy Christians take this line. To be credible before the Lord, we would have to be sure that the God who led us to the job is still with us in it and seek confirmation to that effect. But for a number of people, such as those working in medicine and related professions, parents nurturing young children, those caring for sick family members and others, this may be an entirely appropriate response to the question of choice. But even these groups need to review their motives. It's possible, for example, for a Christian doctor to make God-excluding choices for career gain, rather than for higher motives.

Case 2: "I am totally preoccupied with my career, but I still think it is where God wants me to be. As I have prospered and been promoted, my contribution to God's work has progressively diminished. It's just the way things are; it's my job, you see." The latter phrase is the killer in this case. We often forget in these situations that we have made a series of choices in seeking promotion, more money, more status, and so on. So this accumulation of choices explains our life and work patterns. If we push this line of argument to its limits, there is no time or space left for serving the Lord outside the workplace, and probably a limited amount in work if the "total preoccupation" description is accurate. And there is a real trap here in that the Lord may have allowed us to be greatly blessed in our jobs so that as we became more senior he would have more active witnesses in high places. If this was so, we might be offering him the very inverse of what he was expecting! Think about it.

Case 3: "I became a Christian as a student and I asked God to guide my career choice. In the ten years since then it's been one career disaster after another. Now I think I'll go to Bible college." As it happens, I do know a pastor who says that he finally got the Lord's message and heard his call to go to train in theology after losing his fourth job. So God can lead us by winding paths, even when we ask him to inform our choices. The challenge in this case is to make sure that we don't drift into Christian service when all else fails – unless that is God's lesson for us. He needs us to be truly motivated in all service for him.

God can lead us by winding paths

Case 4: "I am really busy. Come to think of it, I never ask the Lord about jobs. But I do assume that he would have told me if he was not happy with my choices. But things are going great. I'm not sure I want to make a point of asking now. I might not like the answer." Not very Christian, you might think – but it's quite a common perspective. Some of us just do not want God involved in the detail. After all, goes the argument, he did give us the ability to make choices ourselves. The bigger question is whether we can expect to please God without first involving him in the choices?

Case 5: "I do not recall ever making an important choice about any aspect of my life. They all seem to have been made for me, determined by circumstances, or I have drifted into situations. Perhaps it's because I'm not a very assertive person." This is also a rather common experience. People expressing themselves in this way often have a problem seeing that their Christian life has always involved choices. And, beyond that, many people feel rather lost when asked to make an important choice – including the one that lies at the heart of this book. We need God to sharpen our antennae so that we are aware of the choices to be made, and we also need him to assist us in making them to his glory.

Like many people, I have personally been at career crossroads and faced difficult choices on numerous occasions. For me, the first such choice was one of the most influential. Aged eighteen, and with a good school record, I went against all the advice of my teachers and others and chose not to go to either college or university. I was a Christian and I did look for God's guidance in this, but probably in a half-hearted manner. I already had my own criteria and was not as open to advice as I should have been. I chose to take up employment in the steel industry and make this my career. I rationalized that I couldn't make up my mind about which subject to study in higher education and didn't want to waste my parents' limited financial resources. The more I was advised to the contrary, the more determined I became to make my own decision. This was my first practical experience of knowing/not knowing God's peace in a decision. I started my job, and after only a few weeks I knew that I had made the wrong choice. The more convinced I was that I had been wrong, the more I tried to justify my

The more convinced I was that I had been wrong, the more I tried to justify my decision to my peers

decision to my peers. Actually, God's peace in the matter was never there at all. But I did not want to make a complete U-turn, as I saw it. Several unhappy months later, still denying that my choice was the real problem, something very simple happened. I recall literally crying out to the Lord one night, asking him to show me what was making me miserable. And he did this, very quickly, with some considerable force and no small amount of emotion. Perhaps for the first time in my life I wept uncontrollably for several hours, totally convinced that I should have listened the first time. For me, that night was life changing in every sense. I was simply on the wrong track, so I changed direction and subsequently enrolled in university. Looking back at the direction of my career since then, I have often asked myself, "Just how wrong can you be?" Did I benefit from that experience? There is no question that I did, and in many different ways. It taught me to be more serious about guidance for choices, both from the Lord and from wise Christian people; it hurt my pride; and it showed me that there was a very different plan for my life than the one that I was determined to pursue. In the larger scheme of life, such incidents are small but highly influential. Sometimes the first lessons are the toughest!

We have, until now, been associating past career-related choices to current busyness. We have seen that choices set patterns; determine priorities; and can lead to behavior that is different from what we first intended. But this is not the only area in life in which the choices we make impact our Christian service. For example, the choice of marriage partner; professional and business associations; church affiliation; leisure interests, and so on can all be powerful determinants of whether we personally allow Jesus Christ to be Lord. In all of this we should acknowledge the complexity of life – sometimes people make a series of choices before they become Christians that leave a difficult and enduring legacy. God's grace is needed in abundance in many such situations. I have, however, seen a growing number of Christians who do not have such problems and who actually choose to be busy as a defense mechanism against being challenged to be servants of Christ. Sometimes this busyness is as much an excess of leisure as it is an excess of work. The net effect is the same. Satan uses busyness as a weapon to dull their ears to the call of the Lord. Such

God's grace is needed in abundance

behavior suggests that these people have an answer to our core question about whose life it is: "It's mine, thank you." That is, of course, a choice that is open to us: but it is not consistent with naming Christ as Lord. And people who make this choice now must prepare to account for it when the Master asks. When Elijah was confronted by a nation who had yet again become confused about who to worship, he addressed the prophets on Mount Carmel, "How long will you waver between two opinions? If the LORD is God, follow him: but if Baal is God, follow him."[ii] Ultimately, that's what it comes down to. It sounds harsh, but it is biblical. That is the choice all of us have to make.

There is another very serious dimension to this issue. Some Christians make a series of "post-salvation" choices that either diminish or destroy their potential for Christian service. Somewhere along the path of following Christ they took the wrong turn at a crossroads and, when it comes right down to it, they don't want to turn back – at least not right now.[iii] They are aware of the kinds of issues we have discussed in this book, including their biblical basis. They have simply chosen to live their lives by a different set of criteria, to optimize against a different set of variables. Put starkly, it's self at the designer's table, not God. Self-deception leads many such people to forcefully deny that a "choice" was ever made – but we should call it what it is. Many busy people are motivated by money, status, ambition and the social perceptions of who they are (e.g., ego, standing in the community, profession, etc.), as well as by many causes that are worthy in themselves, including family and friends. Among these people who choose to be busy are those who are practiced at explaining why they are in this situation and expert at convincing others about its inevitability. Having discussed such matters on many occasions, and having witnessed the contorted defenses put up to justify such choices, I have long ago concluded that only God can transform such minds. This calls for prayer and reflection, taking time out with God, and reading his word again in order to recalibrate our minds. After all, it's his lordship that is being denied.

> Many busy people are motivated by money, status, ambition and the social perceptions of who they are

---

☑ ACTION:

1. Using the material in this section, identify the critical choices in your past, whether recent or distant, which have had the greatest impact on your ability to serve the Lord.
2. Distinguish honestly between the positive and the negative effects of these past choices.
3. What's the message for you for the future? Is it repentance, avoiding past mistakes, or going forward with a fresh hunger for choosing God's way rather than your own?
4. Which past choices still impact you today as you live with their consequences? Thank the Lord that his grace is sufficient to enable us to continue to serve him, regardless of our mistakes.

What's on my mind? We have thus far thought only about our own choices. We have not yet recalled that, while we chose to follow Christ, that was only *after* he chose us. As Jesus said, "You did not choose me, but I chose you and appointed you to go and bear fruit – fruit that will last."[iv] Note that the performance criterion is fruit, and the question is how much that objective features in our plans. And how focused are we on that goal? Chosen and appointed people need to be careful as to how they occupy their minds – hence the content of this section.

What's going on in our minds is a central determinant of how we live, or don't live, for Christ. Busyness is also associated with preoccupied minds, in which the stresses and strains of everyday affairs compete for attention. The consequences of this are manifold – some physical and some spiritual. The spiritual consequences include an inability to think clearly about the Lord's affairs; inattention to biblical principles; and confusion about life's priorities. Our minds are often so full of details that we lose sight of the big principles by which we are designed to live. On many occasions our concern is with things that are on our minds rather than with what God has placed in our minds. We need to consciously put our minds under the Lord's authority. Paul specifically addresses this issue in a passage calling for discipleship, "Do not conform any longer to the pattern of this world, but be transformed by the renewing of your mind."[v] When our minds conform to the world's pattern, we are influenced by its standards, values and goals – all of which lead us to the wrong answer to the "whose life is it anyway?" question. Paul's assumption is that a renewed mind will have a radical effect on our behavior. John Stott develops this point with some force, "The sequence is compelling. If we want to live straight, we have to think straight. If we want to think straight, we have to have renewed minds."[vi]

Our personal starting point is to acknowledge that Jesus Christ wants to be Lord of our minds. If he has our minds, our choices are much more likely to be in tune with his purposes. In reality, he rarely has – and they rarely are. But this is not a new problem, as we see from the biblical evidence. Paul, writing to the Corinthian church, in which there were many "un-renewed" minds, observed that their "natural" thinking showed up in a number of different ways. These are highly relevant to us as we weigh up past and future choices here.[vii] The Corinthians came to God's affairs with their own bias and had no sense of objectively hearing from him. Their focus was on the visible rather than the invisible, especially when it came to fighting life's battles as Christians. They relied on human strength, not on divine power. They spent much more time listening to human beings than to God. They saw only what was on the surface and rarely looked deeply into spiritual matters. Their state of mind might be ours, or that of many of our contemporaries. When these things are true of us, the world has succeeded in pressing us into its mold. What, then, does it take to get us out of that? Nothing less than the power of God. J. B. Phillips expresses this perfectly, "The modern, intelligent mind which has had its horizons widened in dozens of different ways, has to be shocked afresh by the audacious central fact that as a sober matter of history, God became one of us." Phillips was right – nothing else will do. No amount of cajoling, exhortation or peer pressure will achieve that basic realization that Jesus is Lord. Charles Swindoll wisely said, "Servanthood starts in the mind with a simple prayer of three words 'Change me Lord.'"

Nothing less than the power of God

The Bible makes it clear that thinking and living are inextricably intertwined. Our environment may encourage us to believe in neutral thinking – that it is possible for our minds to be either on idle or separated from what we are and do. The Bible, however, presents our minds as a territory to be possessed for either good or evil. As Paul says, "The mind of sinful man is death, but the mind controlled by the Spirit is life and peace; the sinful mind is hostile to God."[viii] This presents great challenges for us. Who is in control of our minds? Who can help us to unravel the complexities of modern living? Who can deliver us from preoccupations that demand our attention? The answer to all of these questions is the power of the Spirit in our lives. We must find inspiration from the powerful example presented to us in that awesome and unattainable "Christ hymn" to the Philippians. "Your attitude should be the same as that of Christ Jesus," says Paul as he introduces one of his greatest and most moving passages about the Lord.[ix] Oh, to have the mind of Christ, to be able to relate to his strength of calling, to even dimly mirror his conviction! His is a mind that truly expresses the whole attitude and direction of his person. How we need to pray that we come before the Lord with the right attitude. Sometimes we can get the attitude right, even for fleeting moments, but the call is to have both attitude and direction working in harmony at all times. Paul ends this section by pointing to the necessary orientation of a Christian mind: "... and every tongue confess that Jesus Christ is Lord, to the glory of God the Father."[x]

☑ **ACTION:** Listed below are six essential marks of the Christian mind set out by Harry Blamires.[xi] As you read these and review this section, identify the challenges you currently face in aligning your mind to God's purposes.

1. Its supernatural orientation: it lives here , but looks beyond here.
2. Its awareness of evil: a consequence of original sin reaching everywhere.
3. Its conception of truth: based on divine revelation.
4. It accepts that authority of God, which is not a declaration made by an equal.
5. Its concern for the person: recognizing the value of human personality.
6. Its sacramental cast: prone to worship.

Which principles should guide my future choices? As we have discussed both past and ongoing choices that impact the extent to which Christ is allowed to be the Lord of our lives, we have also seen that many factors influence the different choices we make. While it is not possible to reclaim the past, God is always ready to forgive, cleanse and redirect. So we now turn to some guiding principles that can inform future choices. This section looks at three such principles that are not often considered together when making future life-shaping choices – perhaps because they are rather demanding and because we may need to do some radical rethinking in order to address them. Because these principles are also often associated with the handling of wealth, they are not applied to other areas of life.

Tithing: We touched on the subject of tithing in Chapter 3, in our discussion of attitudes to money and materialism. As we have seen, the principle of tithing is based not as much on percentages and money as it is on the attitude of the giver dedicating to God that which is his. Is it not reasonable to dedicate a specific amount of time to Christian work? We know that everything we have belongs to him, but he probably has effective control of very few of these resources. It would be possible to undermine this challenge of tithing with all kinds of arguments, as did the Pharisees. But if we take this ancient principle at face value, is it not wise to consider its relevance for our times? Even to soberly ask the question begins the process of prayer and reflection which creates an openness into which the Lord can speak. What is his reasonable request for our time? What type of work has he equipped us for? What balance does he seek for our lives?

We know that everything we have belongs to him

We should not necessarily measure our response to this challenge of service in the arithmetic of a tenth of our time and effort. It is unlikely to be mechanistic, but it does recognize that in time (the currency of our mortal lives) we acknowledge his supremacy. And, in case the answer scares us, we should recall that this is a master who promised that his yoke was easy and his burden light. Remember, he did not count the cost when he gave up his life for us.

Jubilee: The principle of Jubilee is no less ancient. It was also included in the commands God gave to Moses on Sinai. The nation was instructed to set aside the fiftieth year as a holy and special year. "Consecrate the fiftieth year and proclaim liberty throughout the land to all its inhabitants."[xii] This year was to be uniquely holy – in which radical things happened and normal behavior was changed. For example, resources were to be redistributed among the people and there were to be confession, redemption and new beginnings. This was both a holy year and a costly one, during which lives were significantly changed. Why did God ask them to do this? The Lord said that the Israelites "are my servants, whom I brought out of Egypt. I am the LORD your God."[xiii] Is that not why we are undertaking this reappraisal of our lives and of our service? We are who we are as Christians because Christ rescued us. How, then, do busy Christians in the early twenty-first century respond to this? How many of us have thought that the only way we can really address the questions we have been considering is to do something radical? A change of career; a move to part-time employment; early retirement; job sharing; a total review of time allocation; avoiding the next promotion; taking a year out – these are only a few of the options that come to mind. Of course, they may not be options for everyone. And none of us can wait for the next fifty years to pass before exercising them. But while the early church did not explicitly talk about Jubilee, the spirit of Jubilee was only too evident in the radical changes in the lives of the disciples and in the striking, and much remarked upon, behavior of the early Christians. Is this the time of Jubilee for you? The application of this principle leads some people first to a fundamental employment reappraisal, and subsequently to developing a "portfolio lifestyle," combining part-time secular work with a range of Christian ministries. This is a lifestyle with which I am rather familiar, since it has been my chosen path for the past decade.[xiv]

> *A change of career; a move to part-time employment; early retirement; job sharing; a total review of time allocation*

Fellowship: This familiar New Testament concept is our third principle. At its root, the Greek word for "fellowship" has the idea of commonness. It reflects a spirit not of "what can I keep?" but "what can I give?" It can be used as an economic term referring to business partners. This meaning is reflected in passages such as, "In all my prayers for all of you, I always pray with joy because of your partnership in the gospel from the first day until now."ˣᵛ Living out this principle would require us to consider whether there are specific partnerships in mission and Christian service to which we could contribute – a contribution that has hitherto been withheld due to busyness. This input could take many different forms. It could be practical, involving the skills and experience from our secular employment; it could be financial, deploying the material benefits to which we have access; it could involve prayer and pastoral support, and so on. The heart of the matter is choosing, under God's guidance, to make a new and different commitment for the future – one that is both higher and deeper, and that this time is designed to be for his glory.

The prayerful application of these three principles could transform many of our lives. For those of us who like to be "in control" of our own affairs, this is a hazardous exercise as it involves new levels of surrender. As you consider the implications of not knowing where such an approach to the future would lead, you might find C. S. Lewis helpful. In stepping out with God, he observes, "a glimpse of the next three feet of road is more important and useful than a view of the horizon." Indeed, the guide does not always hand us the whole book of road maps, but in this case God does commit to stay with us for the whole journey. We will return to this issue in the final chapter.

Message 9

1. Take time to think through the implications of these three principles of tithing, Jubilee and fellowship as they are presented above, reflecting on how the Spirit of the Lord might challenge you to apply them.

2. If you are in any doubt about the state of mind that God desires for you as a servant, try reading Philippians 2 once a week for the next year.

3. Reflect on the ways in which your own choices have influenced, and continue to influence, your Christian service – whether positively or negatively.

Further reading

Bradley, John and Jay Carty, *Unlocking Your Sixth Suitcase* (Colorado Springs, CO: NavPress, 1991).

Andreasen, A. Niels-Erick, *The Christian Use of Time* (Nashville, TN: Abingdon Press, 1978).

Stowell, Joseph M., *Eternity: Reclaiming a Passion for What Endures* (Chicago, IL: Moody Press, 1995).

Murray, Andrew, *Absolute Surrender* (London: Marshall, Morgan & Scott, 1957).

Endnotes

i   2 Cor. 10:5.

ii 1 Kgs. 18:21.

iii Some of these "crossroads" choices are, of course, irreversible – and the consequences for the choices we make outside of God's moral will can be painful. It is important to remember the crucial nature of repentance and the fact that there is always a way back.

iv Jn. 15:16.

v   Rom. 12:2.

vi On this topic see John Stott, *New Issues Facing Christians Today* (London: Marshall Pickering, 1999). Ch. 2, "Complexity: Can we think straight?" is particularly helpful.

vii 2 Cor. 10:1-7.

viii Rom. 8:6.

ix   Phil. 2:5-11.

x   Phil. 2:11.

xi   H. Blamires, *The Christian Mind* (London: SPCK, 1963). See also D. W. Gill, *The Opening of the Christian Mind* (Downers Grove, IL: IVP, 1989).

xii Lev. 25:10.

xiii Lev. 25:55.

xiv An enlightening exploration of this can be found in J. Rubery, *More Than a Job: Creating a Portfolio Lifestyle* (Carlisle: Paternoster, 2001).

xv   Phil. 1:4-5.

10
Where Do I Go from Here?

"We are not trying to please men but God, who tests our hearts." (1 Thess. 2:4)

Outline   This final chapter looks ahead in the light of all that we have explored together. We have examined a wide range of biblical teaching related to our lives and our service, and this chapter takes as given that honestly and prayerfully searching for confirmation of our future direction is one of our responsibilities. The chapter addresses the following five questions on this topic.

Whose life is it anyway?
Our central question remains to challenge us, as does the Christian answer to it. We examine the answers that others have given to similar questions. Part of our task here is to try to set out what we intend to do with our lives.

How do I get guidance?
This section looks at both when and why we need guidance in both secular and spiritual life. We will also review the necessary conditions for being open to guidance.

What can I learn from looking back?
This brief but illuminating exercise attempts to summarize our lives so far by identifying a series of symbols that have characterized it.

What are my aspirations for the future?
With the help of three biblical pictures of the Christian, we are able to review how we might adjust our own aspirations for our future behavior.

How do I start?
Accepting that this largely depends on our starting point, this section shares some practical and personal lessons on reshaping our time and resource allocation.

Whose life is it anyway? This is the question that has constantly challenged us throughout the book. While we have noted that the actual behavior of Christians reveals many different answers, there is in fact only one truly Christian answer. Our lives belong to Christ our Lord. As we have observed, however, there is a significant difference between his having ownership and having control. I may own the title deeds of a house but never take possession of it or live in it. We control the right of access to our lives. God has designed us this way, and he has determined our capacity to commit or not commit. We call it choice. As our theme text above from 1 Thessalonians 2:4 implies, our choice is to either please human beings or please God. The central challenge this book presents is for all of us to give our lives back to the owner. It is the call to make Jesus Lord again. At least some of the issues discussed in earlier chapters have probably caused you to think. I know that I have thought long and hard, and these pages contain much of my life's struggle with time and resources. Busyness in its many forms and varying contexts is often only an excuse. But, like many excuses, it feels more like a reason than an excuse because we prefer it that way. John Calvin was right to say that "the gospel is not a doctrine of the tongue, but of life." It is simply not enough for us to claim an allegiance that does not reach into every part of our lives. After all, we are among those who have openly declared "that there is another king, one called Jesus."[i] Consequently, we acknowledge that as Christians we were designed to be Christ-sufficient, not self-sufficient.

It is the call to make Jesus Lord again

While the Bible does not pose our question in these exact words, it does consistently address the underlying issues. Who else has responded positively to our question? Paul did, when he declared, "For to me, to live is

Christ and to die is gain."[ii] This was a powerful summary of his life and an accurate reflection of his motivation and behavior. It's a great sound bite, but it's much, much more than that. And few of us could ever aspire to say it. Peter also responded to this question when he wrote with confidence that, "His divine power has given us everything we need for life and godliness through our knowledge of him who called us by his own glory and goodness."[iii] A lot of our busyness is

All I have is yours, and all you have is mine

directed to accumulating more of something, often under the subtle influence of society's definitions of needs and wants. Is it not salutary to be given this insight into God's complete provision for us? And to see that he satisfies a hunger that we can scarcely understand but often experience? The best answer of all to our question came from the Lord himself. In his prayer for the disciples, addressed to the Father, he declares, "All I have is yours, and all you have is mine. And glory has come to me through them."[iv] Here, then, is the heart of surrender, the words of ultimate commitment that the Lord longs to hear from his disciples – including us. To think that people like us could in any way contribute to his glory!

Not everyone in the Bible who asked this question lived a surrendered life. Many who followed the Lord turned back when it came to the crunch. They simply found his call to follow far too demanding. On one occasion John records many disciples saying, "'This is a hard teaching. Who can accept it?'"[v] Most of us, as Christ's followers, have known for some time exactly what the Lord demands from us. In that sense, there is no hiding place. The disciples above were early leavers who apparently stopped shortly after having started. The Lord, who called himself the bread of life, made it clear that he was not only feeding their bodies. He would also give spiritual food and make demands on their minds and hearts. At that news, they were gone.

It took Demas rather longer. He was once centrally involved in Christian service alongside Paul, Luke and others, but something serious happened. Paul tells us, "Demas, because he loved this world, has deserted me."[vi] For many of us, this is an ever-present danger – not least because a lot of busy people really enjoy what they do (and I count myself among them). But in this case the world's snare caught its man, and he was lost to the Christian cause. It is more than likely that his love for Christ had diminished long before he left. Relationships that are not nurtured just fade away – including those with the Lord.

I will not just live my life. I will not just spend my life. I will invest my life

Christian experience and literature over the centuries has provided the church with countless exemplary cases of dedicated lives, each of whom could provide helpful role models for us. Doubtless many, if not all of them, would have claimed that they were led by the Spirit to find the correct answer to our question and to live accordingly. C. S. Lewis speaks to this subject as follows: "The glory of God, and, as our only means to glorifying him, the salvation of human souls, is the real business of life." As Christians we know that it is, but we often forget that this is so. At times we would benefit from making a simple statement about our mission in life. One such statement greatly appeals to me because of its clarity of intent: "I will not just live my life. I will not just spend my life. I will invest my life." Helen Adams Keller's words set the perfect tone for the rest of this final chapter. Her words express the essence of discipleship as the Lord taught it.

☑ **ACTION:** Prepare a simple statement that describes the intent of your life at the present time. How has your behavior reflected this intent since you became a Christian? If you have been challenged to change this statement of intent as you look to the future, how will it read?

How do I get guidance?   This chapter is primarily about looking ahead. As we do so, we encounter the important question of guidance, to which we now turn. If I want to be guided, whether in the natural or spiritual realm, I have to first answer a question. Do I really want to be guided? We all need to start with the psalmist's pledge, "Since you are my rock and my fortress, for the sake of your name lead and guide me."[vii] Note the assumptions here and whose interests are involved – not just ours, but his as well. There are many Christians whose libraries are full of Bibles and challenging works on discipleship who evidently do not look for God's guidance in many dimensions of their lives. The truth is that we either seek it or we don't – it cannot be done in half measures. It's my prayer that if you have stayed with me to this last chapter, you may be open to the work of the Spirit of the Lord guiding you to a different future. You may be prepared to live as if there is a different, more sacrificial answer to the "whose life is it anyway?" question. Doubtless it will still be a busy, complex and stressful future, but it may be a better balanced one. God does not promise to give guidance to save us the bother of thinking, so we should think about when we need a guide in everyday life. Among these circumstances are the following:

- When we either do not know the way, or do not remember the way.

- When we cannot move ahead with safety.

- When we are afraid.

- When we come to a crossroads and do not know which road to choose.

- When we are lost.

- When we are confused.

- When the assumptions on which we have based our lives are questioned or removed.

It is clear that Christians need guidance in all these situations. Lots of busy Christians have simply lost the way and do not know how to adjust their lives to get back on track with God's expectations of them. Every moment is committed, every calendar page is full. It is also Satan's business to work to encourage amnesia in us and to dull our responses to the challenges that we do receive from the Bible. For some there is a potential set of "hazards" in that they fear the career consequences of not being at every high profile conference, leisure outing, dinner evening with the boss, and so on. Equally, crossroads experiences, with which we are all very familiar, can be bewildering. Busy people often arrive at one of life's crossroads under immense pressure. Fundamental decisions are called for with little time for reflection, and often by people who have little or no knowledge of, or interest in, the Christian's process of checking such decisions out with the Lord. Such decisions made by others might require radical adjustments to personal and family life. In some cases the busy Christian fails to properly consult at both the human and divine level, with dire consequences. The last item in the boxed list above is particularly important. Our fundamental assumptions can be called into question in many situations relating to health, employment, marriage and family, to name but a few, and suddenly what we took for granted is no longer valid. Some of the foundations of life are shaken. What we thought of as being "under control" is in fact out of control, and the future is uncertain. This is not necessarily associated with busyness, but it can be. We can be too busy to see the signs of health deteriorating, relationships under stress, employment conditions changing, and so on. These signs are only too obvious in retrospect, and we can be full of regret and much in need of guidance – the independent becomes dependent. We often need to get to this place before we can really hear God's voice again.

make God's choices in God's way while here on earth

We need guidance in these and many other similar situations. But *why* do we need it? The simplest answer is to enable us to make God's choices in God's way while here on earth. He wants to guide us and has promised so to do. This is regularly confirmed in passages such as "'I am the LORD your God, who teaches you what is best for you, who directs you in the way you should go.'"[viii] Nor is it the Lord's intention to keep us guessing as to which direction he wants us to take or as to whether or not he has a plan. Jeremiah's words are encouraging, "'For I know the plans I have for you,' declares the LORD, 'plans to prosper you and not to harm you, plans to give you hope and a future.'"[ix] Perhaps we should pause here to ask some personal questions. Do I know God's plan for me? Do I feel that my life to date has fulfilled God's plan? Have I looked for recent confirmation of that? If I have looked and found no confirmation, can I trace the events that led to my being "off plan" and on my own plan? Or is it possible that God's guidance featured greatly in the early days of faith, in the establishment of relationships, in the making of career choices, but has rarely been on my mind since?

While our God is a committed guide, we are often not willing to meet his conditions to be guided. Here the real enemy is self, although we often go to considerable lengths to call it by other names. Louis Evely expresses it in this way, "Man is always frightened as soon as he realizes that he loses himself by giving himself. It is a terrible feeling, a leap in the dark." We need to consider two interrelated sets of conditions. None of us can be exempt from addressing them, for they are at the root of actually wanting to be guided by the Lord. As I set them out, let me confess that I have never found any of this easy.

● *Conditions of heart*: attitude, time, patience and dialogue. Our attitudes have to be shaped by the Spirit within us. It is easy to confuse our desired direction with what we want God to confirm, and to hear the wrong signals. Martin Lloyd-Jones is worth quoting here: "The Devil can give you remarkable guidance; there are powers that can counterfeit almost anything in Christian life." And it takes time. Guidance can be instant and inspirational, but more frequently it is a longer and slower process. It is one area of our lives in which we cannot set a time frame that will require the Lord to conform to our busy schedules. As for patience, we have much to do. The reality of this task is captured in such words as, "You need to persevere so that when you have done the will of God, you will receive what he has promised."[x] Then there is the matter of dialogue, initially in personal prayer, but also with wise and experienced people known to us. They should also be encouraged to pray.

● *Conditions of relationship*: obedience and faith. God opens and closes doors for us. One of the biggest challenges for many of us is to distinguish between an opportunity that we are keen to take and one opened up by the Lord. The former may look great and irresistible by the standards of our peers, it may be exactly what we have always wanted, but God might not be in it. Put simply, it may or may not pass the Lord's tests. Paul links our Christian call "to the obedience that comes from faith."[xi] We need to do the same. But there are many situations in which the direction we are to go is not obvious. This is where obedience to the guide, rather than to what appears to be immediate guidance, is crucial. As Martin Luther once said, "I know not the way God leads me, but well do I know my guide." This reminds us that guidance is a continuous process, like traveling along a road that has many milestones and not a few crossroads. Some of us have a nagging doubt about getting it all wrong even after all of this process – in which case we should be encouraged by the "Balaam's ass factor." God was angry when Balaam went with the princes of Moab, "and the angel of the LORD stood in the road to oppose him"[xii] ... "your path is a reckless one before me."[xiii] Just as he was thrown off his ass we have the assurance that, if we've got it wrong, the Lord is capable of stopping us! Just as well.

☑ ACTION:

1. Identify your personal barriers to accepting God's guidance and reflect on them. Take time to set out on paper what you consider God's current plan for you to be.

2. If you are by any chance so busy in Christian activities that you have little time to practice being a Christian, seek God's guidance on priorities once again.

3. God is committed to guide us. Think about the implications of this verse for your next steps, "Whether you turn to the right or to the left, your ears will hear a voice behind you, saying, 'This is the way; walk in it.'"[xiv]

What can I learn from looking back? The world around us often analyzes and appraises the past, complains about the present, and fears the future. Christians are not immune from some of these inclinations, although we should be.

William Shakespeare said that "past and to come seem best; things present worse" – but it is not always so. Having read this book, it is possible that an appraisal of past answers to our central question could leave us with feelings of regret or guilt – or of contentment and confidence. Our feelings are unlikely to be neutral, because one way or another we have all made mistakes in our Christian calling, and we aspire to do better. So what can we learn by looking back?

As a thought-provoking and perhaps novel exercise, let me encourage you to look back at your own life through one particular lens. This is a personal activity that only you can do. Try to recall the critical milestones/ events/activities of your life in the form of a symbol, selecting one symbol for each of them. These symbols may be churches, educational buildings, sports, books, professional artifacts, mottos, geographical locations, specific events, people, and so on. For example, many Christians might want the cross or the Bible as one of their symbols, to recall their coming to Christ. But the choice is yours. The first time you look there may be too many of them. And, if you have done this truthfully, you may not be entirely proud of your list. Some things may have exerted an influence beyond your expectations; other things may not have had enough of an impact. You may need to limit yourself to between ten and fifteen symbols that have been life shaping and have had lasting effects. When you have done this, take one step back and ask yourself what others might choose as symbols of your life, on the basis of their knowledge of you. This is even more difficult, but worth trying. I have been prompted to this thought process by studying the Lord's chief teachings about his death, each of which can be visualized in a symbol. There are at least five of them:

1. *Baptism*: "I have a baptism to undergo, and how distressed I am until it is completed!"[xv] In so speaking the Lord indicates that suffering is integral to his mission.

2. *Cup*: "Can you drink the cup I drink or be baptized with the baptism I am baptized with?"[xvi] This is another reference to a picture of suffering and punishment, something that he alone had to drink.

3. *Road*: "The Son of Man is going the way appointed for him in the scriptures."[xvii] For the Lord, this was a path of rejection and death.

4. *Servant*: "For even the Son of Man did not come to be served, but to serve, and to give his life as a ransom for many."[xviii] He was the fulfillment of the servant king.

5. *Covenant*: "This is my blood of the covenant, which is poured out for many."[xix] The Lord's purpose was to establish a new covenant relationship with those called to his name.

Our symbols are likely to be less momentous than these. In the Lord's case, the cross so dominated his mission and ministry that it is not surprising that these five symbols could well describe his whole life. Indeed, we know that one of the ways in which the early church described the totality of the Lord's life and ministry was as "the way of the cross." As we look at these symbols, we can readily see what they tell us about this man. Our task is to ask ourselves what story our symbols tell.

If we think in this way about ourselves, what does it show us? And what do we learn from it? Knowing ourselves is helpful, but it is often painful as well. Depending on how we have approached this exercise, it might reflect our perceptions of ourselves, past priorities, and the nature of our memories. Among other things, it will highlight the extent to which following Christ has featured in our past. It will provide us with a summary of our life to date, both as we have viewed it and as onlookers have observed it. It could also be a cameo of our past answers to "whose life is it anyway?" In short, this is an exercise in self-assessment that might help us to seek further guidance for the future.

✔ **ACTION:** In the spirit of this exercise, let me encourage you to apply A. W. Tozer's rules for self-discovery to your life. They also help to pick up on some of the specifics of our busyness theme and prayerfully relate them to our central question, so give your own answers to these seven points.

1. What we want most
2. What we think about most
3. How we use our money
4. What we do with our leisure time
5. The company we enjoy
6. Who and what we admire
7. What we laugh at

What are my aspirations for the future? We have discussed Christian goals and objectives in almost every chapter. Practicing a Christian lifestyle, delivering on good stewardship, taking a proper view of work, balancing life's demands, and acknowledging the Lordship of Christ are among the many issues we have considered. In all of this we have recognized the powerful example of Jesus' life and been driven to acknowledge the influence that our practice of Christianity has on our witness. Albert Schweitzer was quite accurate in saying that "Example is not the main thing in influencing others – it is the only thing." Our task at this point is to try to crystallize our aspirations and express them to ourselves in simple terms. One of the best ways I have found to do that is to place myself within some of the New Testament Christian names and metaphors. We have discussed some of these, including stewards and disciples. These names were designed to appeal to people who would reflect on the power of the illustration for themselves. We will briefly consider three further examples below as we seek both to summarize our aspirations and review God's expectations. If these two are separated for too long in any Christian life, the peace and the happiness soon go. These three cited below are also especially relevant for busy Christians.

● *Workmanship*: "For we are God's workmanship, created in Christ Jesus to do good works, which God prepared in advance for us to do."[xx] Although we all have many faults and problems, God made us in his image, gave us life and equipped each of us to live our lives. He gave us life and made us alive and has uniquely equipped each of us for life. But he has also brought us through a range of experiences which have shaped and molded us, making us who we are. One of these experiences is learning to cope with our complex and busy lives. Yes, even in all of that there are forces at work preparing us to be of greater use to the Lord. God's work in us is not aimless, but a product of his design. We are his handiwork, created by God and recreated in Jesus Christ. The aspiration for us is to respond more willingly to the hand of the master craftsman in the future, and thereby to fulfill the purposes for which we were designed and called.

● *Witness*: Paul's commission was, "You will be his witness to all men of what you have seen and heard."[xxi] This mandate was widely given to all Christians in the New Testament, and it is an inescapable obligation for all of us today. It comes with some clear challenges. A witness is someone who must speak from first-hand experience. To be valid, the evidence has to be his own. Christianity has to be a matter of personal experience. And it is only by knowing that we can truly tell. Our personal time in reading and prayer, together with the space for reflection, are some of the things that can get crowded out by busyness – to the detriment of our effectiveness as witnesses. Moreover, a witness must not be afraid to tell what he knows to be true. Distance from the Lord and fear are closely connected. We are reminded of just how real that is when we recall that the Greek word for witness is also the word for a martyr. As Tertullian said, "The blood of the martyrs is the seed of the church." Confession of the lordship of Christ, so critical to our witness and practice today, still leads some disciples to pay the ultimate price. With this picture before us, we would aspire to be a truer, more dedicated, and more active witness in whatever environment we operate.

● *Aliens and strangers:* "Dear friends, I urge you, as aliens and strangers in the world, to abstain from sinful desires, which war against your soul."[xxii] These words describe someone who is a temporary resident in a place that is not his true home. In spite of the feelings of permanence that we sometimes have, this is the reality of our lives. But we try hard to deny it. There are huge challenges in being called by these particular names – especially for busy and involved people. By this standard, the Christian must live as someone on the way to something and somewhere greater – our ultimate goal is God's presence. Enjoy it though we may (and do), we continuously need the perspective that this life is not everything. I regularly forget this, and perhaps you do too. Yet this perspective has to govern our ambitions, standards and values – and, yes, our busyness. This does not, however, mean that this world means nothing to us. We have a clear role to play in it, not least since Christ died for it. We have to move through it with purpose, and we are expected to be engaged in it, but not to fall in love with it. If we took this metaphor more seriously we would aspire to keep all we are and have in better context; avoid the seduction of being deluded by the apparent permanence of all that is around us; and try more seriously to ensure that we fulfill the role the Lord has designated to us.

These pictures are very useful in encouraging us to focus on what we could and should be within each of the varied contexts in which we live our lives. Expressed another way, showing these characteristics is part of the Lord's inheritance in the church that is called by his name. If we pause to think further, however, we can see that parts of that resource get stolen and diverted in other directions. In a passage on the shepherd and his flock, the Lord reminds us of the role of the thief. "The thief comes only to steal and kill and destroy; I have come that they may have life, and have it to the full."[xxiii] The progression is worth noting: steal ... kill ... destroy. One of Satan's regular tactics is to steal and leave something by way of a substitute. Among the things he leaves are materialism, career and pleasure. Yes, God's spiritual treasures can be quietly, unobtrusively, but effectively, stolen. And we can readily be one of them.

How do I start?
This final section offers some lessons from my own experience and that of others to help you take a new approach to your life and attempt to revisit your contribution to Christian service. There is always a hazard in advising how to start, because it all depends on the starting point. Let me assume, therefore, that you have taken the biblical challenges to heart and no longer question why, or if, but how. The motivation is there; it's the pressing practical problems that remain.

● *Work*: Start by revisiting your witness at work, whatever that may involve and whether it is paid or unpaid, in an office, at home, in a school or university. For many Christians, their place of work is an underdeveloped field of service. It is the context in which some or all of your busyness shows itself. It is also an area of huge opportunity. Instead of worrying about how better service is to be "fitted in," why not start where you already are?

● *Personal:* Make sure that you carve out time for regular Bible reading, prayer and study. It is improbable that any of us will get on, and stay on, the right track for God if we neglect this. We need to apply all the usual challenges to ourselves in this area, such as: does it get as much time per week as the newspapers? The board papers? The sports programs? Busy Christians all too often have a poorly developed devotional life.

● *Church:* Reassess your relationship with your church. Accepting that there are short-term and perhaps longer-term time constraints that cannot be readily resolved, ask the Lord and yourself about what service you are uniquely gifted to do. Confirm this with others you trust. See if, by applying this skill set within a narrow time frame, you can make a greater contribution. Some of these skills might be applied to Christian causes in the community or in house groups or seeker classes, where there is perhaps greater time flexibility. Apply the same creativity and flexibility of thought and attitude to this that you daily take into your work environment.

● *Home and family:* This may be where you need to start if this has been the area where the deficit of Christian attention has been the greatest. It's often the first area to suffer from stress and overwork, and the area where the effects are most severe. It would, therefore, be very unwise to take on a new Christian service unless this side of your life is in good order. It could be that your new approach to Christian service was entirely devoted to home and family.

● *Para-church:* I have had many discussions with busy and talented Christians who want to serve but do not know where to find opportunities for their particular skills and time availability. This is a real issue and is often a consequence of living narrowly focused lives, within which people have very specific secular networks and know few Christian people. This can be genuinely frustrating. It can only be addressed by breaking the mold of contacts and becoming more outgoing; checking the web sites of charities; specifically writing to different local and national ministries, and so on. There is a serious dearth of business and professional skills in many Christian ministries. Indeed, the demand far outstrips the supply.

● *Time management:* There is a myth that all busy people manage their time well. Believe me, they often do not. You may disagree, but it is worth looking again at how you use your time and whether there is actually more space in your schedule than you think. It may be a matter of planning in a different way. You might find it helpful to seek advice from other busy Christians who are active in Christian work.

A final word   As Christians we spend too little time considering these matters seriously. We hear few sermons on work, the activity in which we spend much of our lives. This fact, and my own journey with these issues, has been my motivation for writing this book. I can only hope and pray that it will be helpful to others who face these challenges. It is encouraging to see that others are actively developing literature and resources in this important field. For example, I agree with Mark Greene's observation that "contemporary Christians are simply not being equipped for life where they spend two-thirds of their waking time."[xxiv] God can equip us all if we let him. He can also stir his people to represent him better in the workplace.

Message 10

1. Is your answer to the "whose life is it anyway?" question any different now than when you started the book?

2. Keep your mind open to God's guidance. He might already have been offering it for some time. As you look back on your life to date, by what means has God tried to arrest your attention?

3. Have you been honest in representing the symbols of your past life? Or just spiritually correct? If it is the latter, try again!

4. Now that you have finished this book, where will you start to change your future? Draw up an action plan, prayerfully consider it, share it with a trusted Christian counselor, and go forward with God.

Further reading

Campolo, Tony, *Carpe Diem* (Dallas: Word, 1994).

Nouwen, Henri J. M., *The Return of the Prodigal Son: A Story of Homecoming* (London: Darton, Longman & Todd, 1994).

Parsons, Rob, *The Best Decision I Ever Made: Stories of Jesus Changing Lives* (London: Hodder & Stoughton, 1999).

Yancey, Philip, *Reaching for the Invisible God: What Can We Expect to Find?* (Grand Rapids, MI: Zondervan, 2000).

Endnotes

i   Acts 17:7.

ii   Phil. 1:21.

iii   2 Pet. 1:3.

iv   Jn. 17:10.

v   Jn. 6:60.

vi   2 Tim. 4:10.

vii   Ps. 31:3.

viii   Isa. 48:17.

ix   Jer. 29:11.

x   Heb. 10:36.

xi   Rom. 1:5.

xii   Num. 22:22.

xiii   Num. 22:32.

xiv   Isa. 30:21.

xv   Lk. 12:50.

xvi   Mk. 10:38.

xvii   Mk. 14:21 (NEB).

xviii   Mk 10:45.

xix   Mk. 14:24.

xx   Eph. 2:10.

xxi   Acts 22:15.

xxii   1 Pet. 2:11.

xxiii   Jn. 10:10 and see Jim Cymbala, *Fresh Faith* (Grand Rapids, MI: Zondervan, 1999) for his chapter on "Stolen Property," which discusses this issue in some depth.

xxiv   Mark Greene, *Supporting Christians at Work* (London: Administry, 2001), p. 5.

God's payroll
whose work is it anyway?

by Neil Hood
ISBN 1-85078-475-2

Due for release in Spring 2003

Authentic
LIFESTYLE